USING PRESENTATIONS
in Training and Development

Leslie Rae

KOGAN PAGE

London • Stirling (USA)

First published in 1997

Kogan Page Limited
120 Pentonville Road
London N1 9JN
and
22883 Quicksilver Drive
Stirling, VA 20166, VA

British Library Cataloguing in Publication Data

A CIP record for this book is available from the British Library.

ISBN 0 7494 2423 0

Typeset by JS Typesetting, Wellingborough, Northants.
Printed and bound in Great Britain by Clays Ltd, St Ives plc.

Contents

directions; headline planning; horizontal planning; the 'pieces of paper' approach; the patterned-note method; transfer to a working brief; completing a working brief; numbering and tagging each sheet or card; preparation time

Introduction

The number of presentations is increasing all the time: more and more people are being asked to present their ideas, information and so on to wider and more varied audiences. Consequently the demands on such presenters to produce effective presentations is increasing. Many employees for example, who were seen but never heard, are now being forced into a vocal limelight. More people in public and private sector organizations and in voluntary bodies are being required to present plans, information and objectives in a much more public way than ever before. Unfortunately, this increase in public performance has not been accompanied by a proportional increase in *effective* presentations – often the reverse.

Managers in particular are now required to make presentations of a very varied nature – presenting information to a group of staff or at a board or senior managers' meeting; presenting the start or the results of a project; proposing a new product, service or method of working to a variety of audiences; persuading a group to perform as required; being the guest speaker at a company conference; being the expert guest speaker at a training and development course; and so on. Many of these can be very important occasions, not only because of the subject, but through being related to the career advancement of the individual.

More and more selection procedures, particularly for the higher level jobs, take the form of assessment periods, rather than singular interviews. These assessment days can include a requirement on the applicant to make a presentation on either a topic of their own choice or one selected by the organization.

University graduates and undergraduates, in fact students generally are increasingly being required to make presentations about their projects, topics and theses, which have a strong weighting in their overall assessment.

But a more usual and frequent presentation scene is the training and development programme, when trainers are expected to be highly skilled and effective presenters of training sessions and complete programmes. Modern training programmes do not consist solely of 'talk and chalk' input sessions, and consequently the 'presentation' is now more than the trainer facing the learning group and delivering a lecture. Learners demand exacting programmes, presented in interesting ways that enable effective and lasting learning – something rarely achieved by the talk and chalk approach.

Consequently this book is designed principally for use by trainers in the design and production of training events about the use of presentation skills and by managers, coaches and others who need to help people in becoming more effective in presenting.

THE COMMON FACTOR OF PRESENTATIONS – FEAR

Whatever the nature, size and composition of the presentation, there is a common factor among the majority of people required to make a presentation – worry, concern, fear! Speaking in public to a group of people is one of the most stressful activities for most people – including many who are quite experienced at it. The reasons are numerous, but one stands out as the principal reason for this reaction – the fear of making a fool of yourself.

Any fear and panic you may have can be reduced and this book suggests techniques and approaches that will make your presentations as effective as possible. Techniques and methods of presentation in general are common to most situations and the approaches can be applied equally to managers and supervisors; to trainers who have to present an input session to their learners; to secretaries of corporate or voluntary organizations; to students and to the man and woman in the street who have to make a presentation or give a 'talk'.

- The basic approach is a common one – deciding objectives for the event; considerable pre-planning of what you are going to say and how you are going to say it; what constraints or supports exist; what aids you can use and which ones are available; consideration of the most effective means of communication for the particular event; the presentation itself and the most effective techniques for your time 'on stage'; feedback or self-feedback of the success or otherwise of the event. Attention to factors such as these will not ensure complete success, but will reduce the chance of failure, and may just produce an effective presentation!

Some speakers are natural, born presenters, but the majority of us need to learn how to do it and, above anything else, get as much practice as possible, since skill in presentation is not just knowing the techniques. Presenters must practise when learning; give as many presentations as possible; learn from their mistakes; seek feedback on the good and not so good points of their presentations; be as natural as possible when 'on stage', within effective behaviour constraints; and learn how to enjoy being a presenter. The techniques can be learned reading a book, working through a learning package or attending a training course, but whatever the medium, knowledge of the techniques must be followed up by practice, preferably under controlled and monitored conditions in which feedback is available. I have not encountered anyone who was not already one of the 'born speakers' who learned to give an effective presentation solely by reading a book, however good that book might be.

There are few more satisfying feelings than immediately after a highly successful presentation in which you feel you have given your best, and the audience is reflecting a similar feeling.

THE STRUCTURE OF THE BOOK

I have tried to format the material of the book in a logical order, starting with some comments on the feelings of panic when your learners hear that they have to give a presentation. I then consider some of the aspects of communication necessary to ensure that the presentation meets both the needs of the speaker and those of their audience; techniques, methods and models for planning and preparing for the event; actually giving the presentation; and conclude by reviewing performance.

Included are techniques, hints and guidelines for effective present-ations, and many of the chapters also include a number of 'activities' that readers can use themselves or with a learning group with which they are working. These can be selected according to the part of the text in use. Linked with many of the text descriptions of areas of specific advice you will find a 'boxed' summary of this advice. I hope this will save you reference time in deciding whether a particular part of the text is what you are seeking.

Jacqueline Twyman, of First Impressions, contributed Chapter 7, 'Personal Presentation' a subject in which she has considerable experience and skill as a consultant.

A PRESENTATIONS LOG

I suggest that, to help the learning progress, you and the members of your learning groups start with a loose-leaf ringbinder in which can be filed:

- the sheets on which any results from the activities are recorded;
- notes to act as reminders of particular learning points;
- a record of presentations made to be maintained, showing:
  1. from the presenter's point of view:
     (a) the good features
     (b) the features still needing improvement
     (c) a future action plan
  2. the same aspects as in 1(a) and (b) above from comments gleaned from other people – members of the audience, colleagues, the boss, and so on;
- the sheets of a Learning Log completed during the learning event and continued back at work as real presentations are given (the Learning Log is described in Chapter 11).

Presenters should be concerned but not afraid about the prospect of presenting, and when a number of presentations have been given you or your learners may even discover how enjoyable they can be. I am not aware of any deaths resulting from giving a presentation, and that's the worst thing that could happen – everything else is better than this!

ACKNOWLEDGEMENTS

I should like to thank Philip Mudd and Liz Roberts of Kogan Page for the invaluable advice and help that is given so willingly. Jacqueline Twyman not only contributed Chapter 7, but also edited most of the manuscript and made many helpful suggestions.

W Leslie Rae
March 1997

I
—
So You Have to Give a Presentation!

This chapter concentrates on the following key learning points:

- know what is meant by a presentation
- identify the reasons for making presentations
- appreciate the fear aroused when required to give a presentation and consider some of the ways this fear can be alleviated
- know the questions that you need to ask before preparing a presentation, based on the six honest serving men of Kipling – who, what, why, where, when and how.

COMMON FACTORS IN PRESENTATIONS

There are four common factors when you are asked to give a presentation. The first will be your reaction, which is likely (unless you are a *very* experienced speaker) to be one of panic. You may think that this feeling is unique to you, but if you ask your colleagues and friends you will quickly realize that just about everybody experiences this feeling when they have to give a presentation. Even many professional performers who are presenting the words and actions of a play, however long they have been doing it, suffer the same feelings just before taking the stage. However, some people may not have these feelings – again there is no need to worry, but these are the lucky ones.

The second common factor is that the invitation or arrangement to make a presentation is one in which you will have to stand (or sit) in front of a number of people, ranging from one to a thousand. The third is that in the initial invitation or request there will almost certainly be insufficient information on which you can start any action relating to the event without asking questions.

Finally, although the reasons for and the type of presentations can vary widely, the process for completing them effectively is very much the same. If you know how to cope successfully with one type, other types will present few additional challenges.

THE SKILLS OF PERSUASION AND INFLUENCE

Presentations are synonymous with 'communication', and if we can communicate effectively presentations cease to be problem events. But they are far from being *simple* communications, and the frequently required additional skills are *persuasion* and *influence*. Communication is not a one-way process in which the communicator or presenter simply *tells* the audience something, although there are obviously occasions when this is the objective. In training areas little is achieved by 'tell' alone – the audience may have to be told, but they also have to understand, believe and, in many cases, support and accept what is being presented. The bald, 'tell' approach is unlikely to do this without accompanying persuasion and influence.

The key words in persuasion are:

- Attitude
- Values
- Importance
- Credibility

Attitude

The success of your communication rests not only on the attitude you have about the situation and the people with whom you are communicating, but the overt appearance of this attitude. Some presenters can succeed even though they have little faith or belief in the message they are presenting – but they are few and audiences are usually quick to recognize the pretender. If you are internally highly motivated and enthusiastic for your subject, this will be readily transmitted to the listeners who are much more likely to be influenced and persuaded.

Values

Your personal values (such as how you treat people) and your values related to the various -isms are rarely far from the surface, and over a period of time, or in moments of stress, these can surface and become evident to the audience. If these are negative values, they can quickly destroy any rapport you have built up and will reduce your influence considerably, perhaps to zero. For example, if you are antagonistic to particular races or cultures and representatives of these are in your audience, a destabilizing incident might let this antagonism show, however well you might have hidden it to that point.

Importance

How important you show a situation or subject to be will have a strong effect on the listeners. This links with your attitudes – if the listeners develop the impression (rightly or wrongly from your approach) that the subject is not important, you have little chance of persuading them that this is something they should accept. Again, your internal feelings towards the importance of what you are trying to communicate, if allowed to emerge, will have an effect on the listener, much more than an implied importance when this is not your inner belief.

Credibility

So many factors can produce or destroy your credibility with your learning group. Chief among these must be honesty, sincerity and an obvious desire to help them to learn, rather than using them to satisfy your own ego requirements for power and performance. The expert will obviously have credibility when talking about the subject of their expertise, but this will be reduced when the subject is alien to them. The trainer cannot be an expert at everything, but must:

(a) have sufficient knowledge of the subject to enable the learners to learn;
(b) preferably (although not absolutely essentially) have a high degree of personal skill when training in the skill areas;
(c) have, and be able to use effectively, appropriate trainer or facilitator skills.

Without these credibility will not exist and learning through persuading and influencing is less likely to occur. Of course, these skills are much more complex than described above, but if the basic approach suggested is followed, communication with its attendant persuasion and influence will be a stronger candidate for acceptance.

REDUCING THE FEAR

The purpose here is to help you to produce a presentation and reduce any fear and panic you might have. It will not get rid of it completely – no book, learning package or training event can do that, but they do suggest techniques and approaches that help to make presentations as effective as possible. The most important aspect of presentations is practice – the more presentations that you give, the more professional they and you will become, so you should seek as many opportunities as possible even though your mind is shrieking 'No!' One way to overcome fears is to understand them – this will give you some answers as to why you experience fear.

One of the principal reasons why people do not like making presentations is not that they are afraid of making a presentation, but that they are afraid of letting themselves down, making a fool of themselves in front of others. This effect can be reduced considerably by becoming confident and appreciating that:

- the audience knows less than you about the subject (this is almost always the case);
- the audience wants to know about the subject (this is generally the case, although there are exceptions);
- you know the subject being presented (although you need not necessarily be a practising expert);
- you know the best ways to make the presentation and can use them;
- you can make the presentation interesting;
- you are in a position to control the presentation and hence, to a large extent, its success.

The principal aim is to ensure that fear is reduced as much as possible. An important factor here concerns your control of the situation. This has parallels with the fear that many people have of flying – it is usually not a fear of actually flying, but that the plane might crash. This fear is exacerbated by the fact that you have to sit in your seat, passive, and with no control over the situation. Car passengers who are frequent drivers themselves often suffer similarly – they realize that they are completely in the hands of others and have no control themselves. Why are aircraft pilots not afraid of flying? Because they have been trained to fly an aircraft, are in control of it and know what to do if things go wrong. The same applies with the experienced car driver, but not when they are passengers.

It is useful when considering control to think about audience involvement, since as soon as the audience is involved you lose some element of control. You must be ready both to lose some control and be capable of coping effectively with this loss.

PRESENTATION OCCASIONS

Every occasion on which you meet other people face-to-face, especially when you have a specific purpose – perhaps to persuade – is a presentation. The meeting may be with one person – for example, with the boss for an idea or proposal to be put forward; a small group of people – the senior manager group to whom an aspect of work has to be explained; or a hundred people at an open meeting on a particular subject. Although these can appear to be completely different *types* of occasions, as mentioned earlier, all have common aspects and the presentation process is very similar for all. It must be admitted that facing a large group of strangers is more fearsome than sitting with a boss you know, but if most of the factors listed above are present you are in control.

REASONS FOR PRESENTATIONS

Some of the different types of presentations in which you might become involved have been mentioned, but one thing about which you must be certain before embarking on the presentation is the *reason* for the presentation.

The more usual reasons include:

- giving information about a subject
- reporting on your actions and progress in a task or project
- motivating people to take some form of action
- influencing people to accept your proposal or ideas, or to make changes
- instructing people in a new process or other action

The reasons for, or purposes of these presentations appear straight-forward, but circumstances can alter them, and make each type less discrete and specific. If you, the presenter at an information-giving presentation, approach the event with the attitude of 'I know, therefore I'm going to tell them', the event will be that of an active presenter and a passive audience. However, the purpose of giving the information may have the secondary aim of persuading the audience that this is the right approach, motivating them by means of the interest of the information to do something themselves or, by giving the information, enabling them to learn about it rather than simply listen. In such multiple cases the content may be the same, but the personal approach of the presenter must be different. A didactic 'lecture' will do little to change views or attitudes, it will merely inform. A passive audience *may* be sitting listening to your every word – but they may well be mentally on some far South Pacific island! On the other hand, if the audience is involved practically in your arguments, and a discussion rather than a lecture develops, many more effects arise. Involvement and acceptance will produce feedback to you about the extent to which the audience is receptive to the presentation, and hence to your skill.

However, in spite of the above, success is not necessarily completely in the hands of the presenter. Various equations can be quoted. Good material plus a good presenter usually equals a successful event. But good material plus a poor presenter *can* equal failure – however, there can be a positive learning result even in such a case if the audience has an intense desire to know, in spite of the presentation. The ultimate failure will be bad material plus a bad presenter, with a side issue of bad material plus a superb presenter. This latter can ensure a successful event at the time, carried along on the charisma of the speaker, but eventually the audience will realize that all that glittered was not gold.

THE QUESTIONS SPEAKERS NEED TO ASK

When presentations are suggested, you will rarely be given the full information necessary to enable you to start your preparation. Consequently there are a number of questions that you must ask immediately, of both the requester and/or yourself, depending on the circumstances.

If you follow Kipling's six honest serving men (shown below), and ask the questions based on them, this will be a means of ensuring that all the relevant information is obtained.

WHEN?	WHERE?
WHAT?	WHY?
HOW?	WHO?

When and Where?

The 'when' and the 'where' are not the most important questions, but must be asked first. The 'when' may in fact preclude your participation, or the participation of others, as previously arranged appointments may clash. But in any case it is necessary to know exactly how much time is available to prepare. The times of arrival and/or starting need to be known; there is nothing more rude or antagonizing to an audience than late arrival – even if there is a good reason for so doing. The 'where' is essential because, even with the best-prepared material ever, the presentation would be a failure if you went to the wrong location! These may seem simple questions, but it is amazing how often they are not asked until too late.

What and Why?

The 'what' and the 'why' go together. You must be aware of exactly what subject and coverage you are expected to give. Is the presentation simply to describe the superficial aspects of a major project, or will the audience be expecting a detailed, logistic explanation of why it is being done, how far it has gone (and why only to that stage!) and what the future plans may be. Obviously the 'what' also links with the audience aspect, the 'who' that we consider below. So many presentations have failed because the presenter was not clear, or not made clear, about the exact subject they were required to present. Like meeting agenda the statement must relate to the specific reason why the subject is being presented – to inform, to motivate, to decide and so on. In other words the aims and objectives of the presentation must be clear to both you and the audience.

How?

Essential information will be contained in the answers to the question 'how'. How long does an offer give or how much time is available for the presentation? Does it have to be an input only or can the audience be involved? Will there be aids available for use with the presentation? In some cases, how controversial does the presentation have to be? And so on.

Who?

Finally, the 'who' – what needs to be known about the members of the audience? The specific questions you should ask should include the following.

---

1. Who will be there? What is their level, seniority, power? How do I stand in relation to them?
2. What are their backgrounds? Will they be completely unaware of the subject matter, have a little knowledge, have basic knowledge or be very knowledgeable (some may come from an expert area)?
3. How many? Will I be presented with a faceless multitude or a small friendly group? How might this have an effect on my approach or the way I make the presentation?
4. What do they know already about the subject? Have they had talks or instruction on this subject previously? By whom – by me?
5. Will they be really interested in what I have to say or are they there because they have to be? In the latter case do I have to or want to accept this, or can I/should I try to create the interest?
6. What will they expect of me in a wide range of aspects? What will these aspects be – well dressed, a polished speaker, the friendly expert, the salesman, a lecturer or a discussion leader?
7. What is their range of values and prejudices likely to be?
8. Can I produce what this audience will expect of me? A reverse approach is to ask yourself how you might wreck the presentation for them and you – then ensure that you do not.

Level and background

The questions raised in 1 and 2 only minimally relate to your status and personal advancement, rather they are concerned with the mode of presentation. If your audience is inexperienced the complexity, language and level of the presentation will be quite different from that to a group of senior managers with considerable experience, particularly if it is in fields related to the subject of the presentation. Knowing their backgrounds, and especially their experience, will enable your presentation to be pitched at the appropriate level for that group.

Numbers

The principal ways in which group size will affect a presentation will be in the vocal approach and in the use of visual aids. A large group will require a voice projection over a larger area (there may even be a microphone) and careful thought will have to be given to the size of the visual aids if the hall and audience are large. The question of active participation will also have to be considered.

Prior knowledge or instruction

This question links with questions 1 and 2, but is also relevant when the presentation is part of a series (whether or not you have been previously involved) or is instructional.

Interest

Unfortunately this cannot be assumed! The audience may consist entirely of people who want to know, be influenced, motivated or whatever; or they may all be busy people, having to attend an event that given a free choice they would not have chosen; or the audience may be a mixture of these. In the first case, there should be few problems (the number of questions and the desire to be involved might be the major ones), but in the other two the only approach is to try to make the presentation so useful and interesting that their attitudes will be changed. Success is not guaranteed however!

Expectations

These will be linked with and even wider ranging than the interest question. Little interest will suggest low expectations and high interest will certainly be looking towards a high return for their attendance. Will they be prepared to put up with you, because of their interest in the subject, even if you are not a polished speaker? Will their expect-ations change from their first impressions of you 'taking the stage' as a result of visual impact? With a group of formal, smartly dressed business people, how might the appearance of a scruffily-dressed speaker alter their expectations and attitudes?

Values and prejudices

Most people have these, some well under control, others allow them to show. But, particularly if the presentation is on a controversial subject, or the intention is to motivate an uninterested group, or their way of thinking needs to be changed, you must be aware of the objections that might be raised. These may be overtly in the form of vocal disagreement, or covertly with simple non-acceptance of the speaker's views and consequently a waste of their time. You need to be prepared for these and in many cases their guns can be spiked by raising the matter 'from the stage'.

OBJECTIVES FOR A TRAINING AND DEVELOPMENT PRESENTATION

- Be clear about the objectives
- Do they correlate with the identified training needs?
- Do the objectives focus on the real issues involved and what you should be covering in your presentation?
- Is the wording of the objectives clear and can it be universally understood?
- Can the objectives be satisfied within the presentation?
- Are the approaches suggested in the design and planning the most effective and appropriate ones?
- Do pre-programme responses from the learners correlate with the 'official' objectives?
- Be prepared to modify or even jettison some of your personal objectives if they do not agree with the agreed objectives

In the majority of cases where the presentation forms or is part of a training and development event the aims and objectives will have been determined during the training needs identification and analysis (TNIA) process and further refined during the design and planning of the training programme. It may be that that you as the eventual presenter might have been involved in both the TNIA and the planning, so you should be very aware of the objectives and have a copy of them written in a clear and unambiguous document. If the event has been presented to you after these earlier processes, you must:

■ Be clear about the objectives and, if they have been related to training needs, agree that a correlation exists. If the training needs relation has not been made fully, before anything else you must satisfy yourself that the objectives focus on the real issues involved and what you should be covering in your presentation. Make sure that the wording of the objectives is clear and universally understood – do you, the objectives' designer and the learners put the same meaning on them?

■ Ensure that the objectives can be satisfied within the presentation and give initial consideration to the variety of ways in which they can be achieved. If these have been suggested in the planning process, ensure that you agree that they are the most effective and appropriate approaches.

■ Examine the responses to any pre-programme questionnaires sent to the learners to determine what they see as the end result of the programme or presentation. It will be necessary for you to correlate these responses with the 'official' objectives and agree a compromise or change as necessary.

■ Be prepared to modify or even jettison some of your personal objectives if they do not agree with the agreed objectives. The frequent danger is that you may try to inject your favourite topic into the presentation, even though it may not be fully appropriate.

With these cautions in mind you are now in a position to design and plan your presentation, being confident about what you have to include to satisfy the agreed objectives.

SOME ACTIVITIES TO CONSIDER

ACTIVITY: Think about any presentations in which you have been involved, particularly where you have experienced nerves before the event. Identify how these nerves showed themselves and what your feelings were. Write these down in summary form – this is the first step in conquering them.

ACTIVITY: Consider what you think would be a working definition of a presentation that would cover most presentation situations. Write this down and discuss your definition with your group. Amend your definition if necessary, come to an agreed group definition and be prepared to present it to the full group.

ACTIVITY

1. Consider your feelings if you fear, or are very concerned about giving a presentation in front of others – strangers, peers, colleagues, friends, staff, etc.

Try to identify 'why' by asking yourself such questions as 'What am I really afraid of? and continue asking yourself this question until the root cause of any fear is determined. Once determined, you may be able to do something about it; if not, at least you know why you are afraid!

2. Discuss the feelings you have identified with your group and consider the commonality of the reasons.

3. Write down these reasons and look on them as part of you presentational objectives – the ones you will try to conquer or reduce.

ACTIVITY: Think about and list on a sheet of paper all the reasons you can think of for why and where presentations are undertaken. In which ones are you likely to be involved? What do you know about the other situations and can you be sure you may not be involved in any of them? Why are there different presentation situations?

Discuss your views with the rest of the group and prepare a combined, summary list for presentation to the full group.

ACTIVITY: Identify, list and consider the questions that a presenter needs to ask at an early stage about the presentation audience. This will not refer to a particular audience, but the questions to ask about potential audiences in general.

2

Planning the Presentation – I

This chapter:

- considers methods for holding the audience's attention
- identifies the problems of memory and retention of presented material
- suggests various techniques for overcoming communication problems
- describes an effective structure for planning and preparing presentations
- describes how to decide on the principal material to be included and the logical process of the presentation
- gives guidance on effective presentation approaches and styles.

EFFECTIVE FACTORS IN LEARNING AND ACCEPTING

Presenting is not just about giving an effective presentation – the problems of learning, memory and recall of the audience must also be taken into account, otherwise the most superb presentation will have been wasted. One consideration is the need to decide the most appropriate and effective vehicle for presentation. Sometimes the subject will immediately suggest the path, but at other times this way may not be so clear. An introduction to this consideration is provided by a saying attributed to Confucius which describes the basic working of the human mind.

> Tell me and I forget
> Show me and I remember
> Let me do and I understand.

The aim and objective of most presentations is to ensure that the messages given are not only remembered, but also understood. This suggests that 'doing' is probably the best way of understanding the presentation. It is obviously not always possible for the audience to *do* something, but recall is much stronger if this can be arranged.

THE ATTENTION SPAN

Ask yourself 'To what extent do I feel that I am as receptive, am reading and am learning as I was at the start of the book?'

The reason for this question is to introduce the concept that, in addition to the presentation having a basic objective of putting over the requisite message and ensuring it is understood, the next general objective must be that following the presentation the audience will go away and remember what they have heard. In order to do that they must have listened to the presentation, and we have already considered a number of personal and often individual barriers to this attention.

In addition to all the personal barriers, anecdotal accounts and research show that, even with a fully motivated audience, there is a problem of the span of attention during a presentation. People can listen completely for only a certain period of time, at a reduced level for a further period, followed by either minimal attention or complete withdrawal. So you must be prepared to accept that there is a finite time during which learners will listen to your presentation with full attention and plan your presentation and its format and structure accordingly. In the majority of cases, research shows this attention span appears to be about 20 minutes. Obviously the exact length of the period will vary depending on a number of factors – the complexity of the subject, the motivation of the audience, the charismatic approach of the speaker, the time of day, the part of the week and so on. But, after the introduction period, attention starts to wander and reduce over a descending curve, usually only to return for a little while before the known end of the session – the learners anticipate the end of the session and come to life. The point when attention starts to reduce will vary considerably depending on the nature of the subject, its complexity, the motivation of the listeners, the skill of the speaker, etc. Again, the onset of this reduced attention is the subject of various assessments or guesses; under 'normal' situations it usually ranges from 10–15 minutes or so. But although there is no accurate, universal measurement, you can be certain that full attention will last little longer than 15 minutes, and usually somewhat less. It then falls off quite rapidly until near the close of the presentation when the listeners realize that it is almost over – particularly if lunch follows!

A useful rule of thumb, if you are presenting information material, is to talk for no longer than 10–12 minutes before changing the tempo of the presentation. At this stage, a question to the whole group might be posed, or a sub-group discussion or task-solving activity introduced to reduce the passivity of the learners. A video might be shown – advise the group first that they will be performing a related activity (perhaps an analytical discussion) following it; or a different aid – audio or visual – can be introduced. Impact events should occur throughout the session at relevant points, the longer the session, the more frequent and impactive the events. If the session is a particularly long one that does not lend itself to natural changes, as suggested above, it can frequently be helpful to introduce 'artificial' changes.

The long session can be divided into sections, the divisions being made at points that are as natural as possible. During the breaks, if there is no natural activity the learners can follow, a non-related ice-breaker or session-shaker can be used. Some presenters involve their groups in physical activities during these breaks. These not only have the effect of relieving muscles and changing the scenario, but can also reduce any stress that may have built up: running up and down the stairs in the building; a trust walk; an outdoor game – these and others have all been used with effect. But the principal criterion is that a change must be introduced which will break the inevitable pattern of reducing attention.

I have not encountered any research that takes into account the use of presentation aids in this area – visual or audio-visual – but these must interrupt the downward slope and revive the listeners' interest, if only for a short time! A further reminder, if such be needed, that a talk alone achieves very little.

One possibility suggested by this attention pattern (and some experts recommend this as an almost universal rule) is that, because attention appears to be greatest in the early stages and less in the closing stages, the most important messages should be given at these times. A practical application of this might be, if you are discouraged by the 'fact' that much of what you have said in between these stages may have little attention paid to it and certainly has little chance of being recalled, to end your presentation with a strong summary, much stronger and impactive than the usual, simple summary.

MEMORY AND LEARNING RECALL

In addition to the difficulties produced by the audience's attention span and those personalized by the learners, there are other problems of communication in presentations. Most of these affect most learners to some degree and the effective presenter must be aware of them and possible remedial actions.

One of these is the problem of memory retention and recall over time of material learned. Various research suggests that the extent to which learning is recalled over the short period of one day is normally little more than 20–25 per cent. Beyond that, depending on other circumstances, there is a further falling-off in information recall which may in time reduce to zero. One frequent assumption implies a 10 per cent retention after a year. Obviously this recall can vary considerably depending on the subject, the environment, the skill of the presenter and, more particularly, the amount of use made by the learner of what has been learned.

The amount of recall fall-away in such a short period of time is alarming, but unfortunately only too real in many cases. There will naturally be individuals whose intrinsic recall skill permits a much greater amount of retention, but equally there may be some with even less than that shown. This, of course, is not the full story, but it represents what happens both on so many presentation occasions and when retention is taken for granted.

One key solution to this undesirable situation is repetition of the learning at intervals designed to reinforce the memory and recall powers, linked with other approaches to support the repetition. Some of the strategies used in this process can be summarized as:

- Impact
- Structure
- Linked items
- Progressive reviews and summaries
- Post-presentation reminders

Impact

Events, information, etc are normally remembered much more easily if something accompanies them to give an impact, helping the individuals to consolidate the data. This impact need not be explosive, but it should be sufficiently different from the norm to be outstanding.

Structure

If you structure your presentation in a logical, easily-to-follow pattern, the listeners need concentrate only on what is being said, without the added complication of trying to sort out a pattern or logical path. A statement at the start of each section about the content of what is to follow alerts the audience to the material and prepares them to receive it, rather than their being subjected to an unannounced change of topic.

Linked items

If a series of isolated bits of information are presented which are either unconnected or sufficiently different (even within one subject) as to appear to be singular topics, recall will be that much more difficult. Some items will be recalled – the ones the learner is most interested in – but these may not be the ones the presenter *wants* to be recalled. Linking a series of information or ideas will help the listener to associate the total information and make recall easier. An example of this linking is in the memory technique of making up a progressive story using the singular items to be remembered.

Progressive reviews and summaries

One piece of good advice for making a presentation is: 'Tell the audience what you are going to tell them; Tell them: Tell them what you have told them'. In this approach you are trying to ensure that your learners remember and can recall much more than the minimal amount by reinforcing through repetition. An essential is a summary at the end of the presentation, with shorter, sectional summaries as the presentation progresses. A question period after the presentation also helps to reinforce the message, or a discussion for the audience members to describe their views of the material. Reminders of this nature are essential to ensure that a maximum amount of the communication is understood, stored and remembered, and can be recalled. If the presentation concerns some action that the audience will need to implement back at work, early implementation will act as a further, strengthening reminder.

Post-presentation reminders

In almost every presentation situation, on whatever subject, the criterion must be that reliance cannot be solely on the initial presentation or demonstration – the key points, preferably presented in an impactive, interesting way, linked in a logical sequence, must be followed up with reviews, ideally in a varied way. This follow-up should be over as long a period as possible from the event, through to and beyond implementation. Consider the relevance of issuing some form of handout or reminder sheet to help this recall process – but do not rely on this being read. Handouts are notorious for being put in a drawer and forgotten. Usually this is because they are long, complicated and uninteresting. Experiment with novel, eye-catching handouts that have a much greater chance of being re-read and used.

MEMORY AIDS

The strategies identified above will go some way to ensuring that messages are retained for recall. There are a number of techniques that are presented as infallible aids to memory. My experience has been that some work for some people, some for others, some for everybody and some do not work at all! If it is possible to structure the communication to make use of some of these techniques, the audience may find retention and recall so much easier. Remember that an audience cannot be *made* to remember; this is one of their internal mechanisms that only they can operate. All you can do is to use some techniques that will make them want to trigger their memory mechanisms.

These are some of the techniques about which you may have heard or indeed used.

- Acronyms
- Alliteration
- Phrases
- Rhymes
- Pictures/cartoons
- Making a story
- Humour
- Digestible portions
- Repetition

Acronyms

Many people find that they can remember short acronyms which then act as triggers to longer pieces of information. An acronym is a word formed from the initial letters of other words, usually a list of ideas and so on. Many people unused to acronyms use or recognize them without realizing this: one that is relevant to presentations is KISS.

Keep
It
Short and
Simple

It is more effective, although not always possible or necessary, for the acronym to be related to the concept being presented. Otherwise, like KISS, an impactive easily remembered acronym can be used. Even acronyms that are not real words are acceptable in certain situations; the computer industry is very prone to this with GIGO – garbage in, garbage out – and WYSIWYG (pronounced 'wizzywig') which identifies 'What you see is what you get'.

If, during your presentation, you have a particular concept you want the audience to remember more easily, present it in the form of an acronym, reinforced by some of the other aids to remembering, eg repetition. Many people, however, find problems with acronyms, in that although they remember the initials of the acronym, they forget what the initials denote. This is particularly true if the acronym is used only infrequently; frequently used examples become firmly embedded in the memory – a practical example of the benefit of repetition in learning recall. A useful approach practised by several trainers is to list the acronyms they know and use and at regular intervals re-read this list, re-memorizing their meanings.

Alliteration

This approach can be used where an acronym is not suitable or convenient. Here is one example I shall be using later in this book – the four **P**s:

> **P**roject your voice
> **P**ronounce your words carefully
> **P**ause frequently
> **P**ace should be varied

Again there can be a problem of remembering both the alliterative series of letters and what they signify. Repetition and frequent use are the principal methods of helping to solve this problem.

Phrases

Similar to the acronym and alliteration techniques is the use of an easily remembered sentence or phrase, the first letters of each word acting as the trigger of what is to be remembered. An astronomical example of this is intended to help recall the sequential list of star types: O, B, A, F, G, K, M, R, N, S – the phrase is **O**h, **B**e **A** **F**ine **G**irl, **K**iss **M**e **R**ight **N**ow, **S**mack!

Rhymes

Information presented in an easily remembered rhyme can help retention and recall. Probably the best-known examples of this are the rhymes used to remember the days of the month: '30 days hath September, etc'; and to remember weather signs: 'Red sky at night, etc'. If you can construct a rhyme to enable your audience to remember part of your presentation, use it, but do not expect everybody to use it or even remember the rhyme – some people are averse to rhymes.

Pictures/cartoons

The previously quoted words of Confucius are relevant in this discussion of memory triggers, particularly 'show me and I remember'. There is considerable anecdotal and validated research to show that people remember more from a picture than from words – words plus a picture can reinforce this even more. This is why the use of visual aids in presentations is so strongly advised. These visual aids wherever possible should be in the form of a picture or drawing or some other graphic form instead of projected words; or the two media can be combined. Cartoons – preferably humorous – are particularly striking forms of visual aids to ensure impact. The computer and the many DTP packages that contain clip-art images and cartoons have made this approach much easier for those who cannot draw. But whichever type of image you choose, make it as striking as possible without going over the top, and its impact will help the audience to remember the points.

Making a story

This is my own favourite method of remembering a list or collection of facts or items and stems from Kim's Game, in which a trayful of objects is remembered. If, for example, I want to remember the items – toy car, jumper, wall, garden, flowers, house, vase – I could construct a little story that goes 'I jumped out of my car that all my friends call a toy, climbed over the wall into the garden and picked some flowers before going into the house to put them into a vase'.

Humour

The rationale behind using humour to help people remember something is that if they can have a laugh they are relaxed and enjoying themselves. Consider the people, places and incidents you can recall easily – most of these will be the enjoyable experiences in your life, we tend to filter out of our memory the unhappy ones. So if you want to make a particular point in your presentation that you feel is significant and should be remembered, introduce humour into its description. This does not necessarily mean telling a joke, and certainly not an irrelevant or unacceptable one, but perhaps an anecdote that includes the point clearly, or relates the point to a humorous event in which you were involved.

Digestible portions

KISS has been referred to earlier as an acronym, but it also represents a useful technique for helping people to remember. Complex and prolonged monologues are difficult to listen to and to remember, so a short, uncomplicated description will make much more of an impact. Even complex items will be possible in this system by breaking them down into smaller, digestible portions. How do you eat an elephant? In bite-sized chunks!

Repetition

Of the more standard approaches to helping people remember what you have said, repetition is probably as effective as any of the others. The recommendation, underlying a summary of what is to come at the start of the presentation, one during the event about what has happened so far, and another at the end to wind the event up, is their practicality. Another repetitive approach is to make the same point several times, but expressed in different ways and perhaps using one of the other techniques described above. The technique mentioned earlier of 'Tell them what you're going to tell them; Tell them; Tell them what you've told them' is another effective application of repetition.

But ensure that you do not overdo this or, of course, any of the other techniques, or the reverse of what you wanted may occur because people will realize what you are doing, or become bored with observed repetition, or feel that they are being patronized.

THE PLANNING PROCESS

Thorough planning for a presentation is a 'must' for the development of your skills in making presentations, since planning is the linchpin on which any presentation relies. The more preparation time you are able to afford the better, but there are ways in which the optimum use can be made of whatever time is available.

Planning and preparing a presentation can best be achieved by following a logical structure, at least until the presenters are more experienced and skilled. The structure I commend has 12 stages:

1. Define or confirm the nature and purpose of the presentation – ie the aims and objectives
2. Analyze the potential audience
3. Decide on the principal material and logical process of the presentation
4. Decide on the presentation approach and style
5. Plan the presentation and prepare the brief
6. Decide on and produce the relevant aids – visual or audio-visual
7. Prepare any handout material
8. Rehearse the presentation
9. Make any necessary modifications
10. Prepare or assess the environment
11. Make the presentation
12. Review your performance

Items 1 and 2 are covered in depth in other publications, and I therefore discuss them only briefly here. The remainder of this chapter discusses items 3 and 4 from the list.

AIMS AND OBJECTIVES

The possible reasons for making a presentation are discussed elsewhere, but you must ensure that you are completely certain in your own mind why your presentation is to be made. This is particularly important when the decision for the presentation came from elsewhere and the programme planning has been made by others. The questions you should be asking yourself should include:

- Is the intention simply to inform or will an idea have to be sold to the audience, influencing them so that they are motivated?
- Is the presentation part of an instructional programme, in which case the relevant techniques will need to be part of the presenter's repertoire and a completely different form of presentation may need to be given?
- Is the presentation to be a report – and if so, to whom?

When you are actually preparing for a presentation, once its objectives have been determined (and even if they have been recorded elsewhere), it is useful to write them down on a sheet of paper and fix it prominently so that it can be seen while the presentation is being designed. This visible prompt will constantly remind you of the planned objectives to which the presentation design should be moving.

AUDIENCE ANALYSIS

This subject was introduced in Chapter 1, but its importance cannot be overstressed. Too often the potential presenter is so concerned about the presentation itself that the actual audience is forgotten about. As we have seen, the variety of audiences with different needs, attitudes, levels and reactions requires the selection of approaches and techniques that will best suit that particular group – or as far as any disparate group can be satisfied! This audience analysis must be kept firmly in mind, particularly in the later stages of actually preparing the material.

A number of aspects should be considered and will include:

■ How many people will be present? This will obviously have an effect on how the event must be arranged.

■ What will be the age range of the audience? This can have a significant effect on the final and detailed planning of the event and also who might be involved. New entrants, the young or inexperienced will require a different approach to existing, older, experienced people.

■ With what level of knowledge will the learners be starting the session? Again the ideal will be to have pre-knowledge of this and there should be data resulting from a needs identification – this will probably show, except in the case of completely new work with which none of the people could have had previous experience, that there is a range of levels. This obviously will produce problems for the presenter in terms of where to pitch the event – too low, to suit the ones with little skill level, and the more skilled participants will be bored. Pitch the level too high and the lower skill level learners will not learn and may cease trying to do so. However, although most programmes have to cope with a mixed range, every attempt should have been made in liaison with the line manager to select participants for particular events on the basis of level.

SELECTING THE MATERIAL

The presentation will be on a subject about which you are either an expert and know a considerable amount, or one that you will have to research to build up sufficient knowledge to avoid making a fool of yourself. Remember the earlier acronym – KISS: keep it as short and as simple and as appropriate to the situation as possible.

We always tend to include too much material, mainly because we are afraid that we may run out of material rather than have too little time, whereas in the majority of instances the reverse is true.

However, in spite of this advice you would be wise to 'have something up your sleeve'. Before a presentation, unless you know your audience very well, you can never be sure how much they know about the subject. Soon after starting your presentation you may become aware that a significant proportion of what you were going to say is already known by the group and to go ahead would decrease the impact of your event. So, have in your 'toolkit' a range of material that you can use to replace the original material – this must, of course, be relevant material. If all your presentation content has been covered, a valuable alternative, depending on the subject, might be a related activity, a role play, a problem-solving case study and so on.

You do not need to be concerned that you will get this exactly right – very few, even very experienced presenters do. However, it is useful in the early stages of the planning to start with more material than will be used, so that a weeding-out process can take place, rather than a frantic search for more material.

Fortunately there are techniques that help to balance the amount of material for the presentation itself. One of these is concerned with allocating priorities to different parts of your presentation content. The final allocation will come later, but at this stage every potential presenter should be aware of the:

Must know
Should know
Could know

approach. The possible material for any presentation will fall into one of these groups.

Must know

This is the type of information that is essential for inclusion in a presentation. Without it a talk would have little meaning.

Should know

This information would be very useful for the audience to hear, but if all the time had been taken up with the *Must knows* and this further material had to be omitted, the presentation would not suffer too much. However, it would be preferable to be able to include this material.

Could know

This is the material that would be included only if there was some additional time available. It is not essential, albeit perhaps interesting and useful, and could safely be omitted if necessary.

CONTENT RELEVANCE

One of the principal blunders in making a presentation or presenting a training session is to fail to ensure that your material is up to date, authoritative and correct. Your audience will anticipate and will expect your material to be up to date – if it is not, your credibility and that of the event will be lost. If some parts are incorrect, there will be a growing suspicion about the veracity of the remainder of the material or your personal credibility. Ensure that your material is as up to date as possible, and it helps to increase the impact of an event if you can add – and make a point of this in presenting it – something that is very new about which the audience will not be aware, but will have a direct effect on them

SESSION DESIGN

Type of approach to be used

The first, and probably the most important decision, concerns the type of approach that will be used to satisfy the agreed objectives for a particular group of learners: subsequent decisions will follow on naturally from this.

Presentation approach and style

How analysis of the subject and the audience is approached and the methods and techniques to be used will depend on the results of the work in the first two parts of the preparation structure. But decisions on the actual approach and style (or styles) you will use must be made at this stage, otherwise there is a danger that you will walk into the presentation unprepared for what awaits you. To help this process you should be asking yourself some questions.

- How can I avoid patronizing the group that is ignorant of the subject?
- How can I avoid antagonizing the group that has considerable knowledge of the subject?
- To what extent will I invite, encourage or discourage participation during the presentation itself?
- Is the environment conducive to using presentational aids?
- Are these aids available or can they be made available? Can I use them effectively?
- Is the issue of a handout relevant in this instance? What kind? How will it be produced? In what format? When shall I hand it out?

From previous experience or from other feedback or appraisal comments that you have received, a decision can be made at this stage about which presentational style is going to be the most appropriate for this event. If it seems that there might be some shortcomings, enquiries and arrangements can be made for development of this aspect.

Obviously, until the more detailed preparation aspects are reached, you will not be aware of every type of approach that will be needed or is possible, but some advance consideration and preparation at this stage will avoid panic stations later on, perhaps too close to the event for effective action.

Time constraints

The question of the effect of time constraints is one of the major factors in the design process.

The first feature is the possible conflict because of a constraint on the time available for session. This constraint might be imposed without consideration of the needs demonstrated by the TNIA – 'You have X days in which to run a training event'. In such cases substantial restrictions are placed upon the design of the sessions that need to be included. Irrespective of the total needs identified, decisions must be made about which of the needs must be included. The earlier prioritization of the objectives will help in this instance, whether this is based on importance of the subject or on the widespread nature of the deficiencies.

The alternative approach would be for the session designer, taking into account the identified needs and the minimum priorities from these needs, to propose and fight for a length of time that would be sufficient to mount an effective programme.

In most cases a compromise will be the normal result – a not quite sufficient time to make the session a fully effective one, but one not so constrained as to make it almost a non-event.

PRESENTATION METHODS

Presentations are rarely straightforward talk-and-chalk by the presenter nowadays and frequently include a range of approaches that depend on the presenter's skills, the needs shown by the objectives, the audience attitudes, etc. Much of the decision-making on the methods to be used will fall to the practitioner responsible for sessions, but the programme designer may also have a say – hopefully this results in agreement between the designer and the practitioner. The overall time available will be critical – it may be desirable to include x number of experiential activities within the session, but because of the time required for these their number must be limited to the ones that will carry the most significance.

The wide range of possible methods includes the following, although some are suitable only in training and development.

- Presentation sessions/Lectures/Input sessions (or similar descriptions for activities of this nature)
- Buzz groups
- Syndicates
- Discussions
- Demonstrations
- Question and answer sessions
- Case studies and simulations
- Role playing
- Activities
- Videos
- Computer-assisted training (CAT)

PRESENTATION SESSIONS

The presentation session, in its many guises, represents the most common method although in many cases it is not the most appropriate. In their basic form they are 'tell' events, in what is traditionally described as a *lecture*. In this form the presenter or other expert speaker talks to (or at) the passive audience, which is expected to note the many words of wisdom and learn from these. As described earlier, the restricted attention span of a passive audience can work against this method.

As it is probably the easiest type of approach, it may be used on too many inappropriate occasions, although there are situations in which, presented in an effective and appropriate manner, it is the correct one.

But current views of acceptance and learning suggest that this is probably the most ineffective form of learning, although it can be improved by the addition of supportive or supplementary techniques, such as session aids, discussion, videos, activities etc. Otherwise, presentation sessions should be limited to a maximum of about 15–20 minutes. Even the use of visual aids, however, can improve this situation and extend the length of the audience's attention span. If there is to be a multiple style approach, the 20–30 minute maximum need not be adhered to, although any one session should really last no longer than 45 minutes to one hour. The exact length will depend on the nature of the various component parts of the session, the complexity of the subject and the likely motivation of the learners. Initial design might suggest a session which could follow a pattern of:

A brief introduction to the subject	up to 5 minutes
Input by the presenter, oral presentation supported by visual aids	up to 20 minutes, but preferably 15
An activity related to the subject to give the learners the opportunity to practise what has been learned	an activity of 15–20 minutes
A feedback session on the activity	about 15 minutes
A summary of the session and the lessons learned	up to 10 minutes
Total time for the session	about 65 minutes

This example considers a relatively simple subject content, and time for the constituent parts has been cut to the bone. You will note that, even so, the approximate time required is just over an hour – effective training takes time, and it is better to reduce the amount of learning material to ensure its effectiveness than to try to cram too much into a constrained period.

BUZZ GROUPS

One effective supportive technique during input sessions is when the presenter, having reached a pre-planned point (preferably before the decreasing attention watershed), poses a question to the learning group or, having made a statement, asks them to consider it. Frequently it is not convenient or desirable for the group to discuss the topic as a full group or to leave the room to do this, so the technique known as 'buzz group' is introduced. The learning group is asked to break up into smaller groups – say, in a group of 12 learners, into four groups of three learners each – by moving their chairs into these sub-groups. The 'buzz' becomes evident as up to 12 voices can be heard discussing as requested.

Usually groups are asked to buzz for short periods – five or ten minutes. If this takes place early in the course when individuals may not be keen to speak out in public you can suggest that a spokesperson is elected from each group. The spokespersons then, when the full group is reconvened, give, neutrally, the sub-groups' views or responses.

SYNDICATES

A syndicate is an extension of the buzz group approach and is sometimes referred to as a task sub-group or a breakout group. Usually a learning group, either during a presenter presentation or at the end of it, is divided into smaller sub-groups and given a task to complete. The syndicates are allocated separate rooms where they can work in private before returning at the end of the allotted time to the main group, and what is referred to as a plenary, review or feedback session is held. During this the observations of the observers (if any) are given to the participants, followed by a general discussion on the activity and the lessons learned.

The task given to the syndicate can be a problem-solving, decision-making task; a views and opinions gathering exercise; or a management or other skill exercise, game or activity. A specific time in which to complete the task is usually allocated and, in meeting or leadership training events, a group leader is selected or the group is asked to elect a leader.

DISCUSSIONS

Discussions are very common and very useful learning techniques to include in a presentation session, whether they have been planned (essential in a constrained session) or have occurred naturally. They have the value of actively involving the audience, giving many the opportunity to speak and enabling a wide sharing of information and views.

Unplanned discussions must be controlled strictly by the presenter, otherwise some material may have to be omitted. Deciding whether to omit material (however important), should be viewed in relation to the impromptu discussion started by the participants, which may suggest interest in that particular topic.

DEMONSTRATIONS

Demonstrations add additional interest to a presentation and are very useful, practical methods of either showing the learners a piece of equipment or another operation and how it works. Obviously much will depend on the size and availability of the piece of equipment or complexity of the operation, but this may form part of the introduction to the session, or be used progressively as the session develops.

Demonstrations of more general skills, such as people skills, are much more difficult and indeed may present dangers. If the demonstration is, for example, of a negotiation, there is the danger that the learners will see this as 'this is the way you *must* do it'. If it fails in some way, the credibility of the approach becomes suspect in the minds of the learners. A video that represents a neutral demonstration of skill and which may in fact be a vehicle for criticism by the learners is much safer and more useful.

QUESTION AND ANSWER SESSIONS

These too may be deliberately included in sessions (though rarely as sessions of their own), preferably occurring naturally. They are techniques that must be handled with care, as too easily the questioning can become an interrogation or even a put-down of the responders, with the consequent withdrawal of their involvement. A friendly approach is 'What do you think?', 'Why do you think that?', 'Would you do it any differently?' and so on.

CASE STUDIES AND SIMULATIONS

These are techniques and approaches that can form part of a session, although their inclusion suggests that a substantial amount of time is available, as they are time consuming.

Case studies are problem-solving activities, usually more complex than the traditional group problem-solving activity or game. They can be long or short, simple or complex and, unlike many general problem-solving activities they are directly job related, being constructed from actual events that have occurred in organizations.

A *simulation* is an extended case study in which the learning group becomes a simulated company, or group of companies competing with each other, behaving as far as possible as the company managers. All the necessary background information is provided initially but, particularly if a computer is available, additional database and spreadsheet data for which the group has to search, having identified that it needs further information, is also provided. Individuals are given, or select from within their group, the roles of managing director or chief executive, financial director, sales and marketing director, production director, personnel and training director and so on. The group is given a time in which to solve a number of problems or otherwise exist as a company, with the objective of making a profit over a sum given to them at the start. Many variations of this type of simulation are possible and the time allocated can be extensive.

Simulations are not usually associated with presentation sessions because of their complexity and time consumption, as both case studies and simulations can form complete training courses in which all the training objectives and learning points have been included. However, this should not deter the session designer if sufficient time is available for these effective approaches to be used.

ROLE PLAYING

This is one of the two most widely used activities in training courses (although less common in presentations) and provides the learners the opportunity to practise, in conditions simulated to be as close to real-life as possible, the learning they have achieved. In a similar way to case studies and simulations, role plays can either be linked with or be integral parts of presentations. Usually the role plays are related to interviews – counselling, grievance, discipline, appraisal, selection, termination and so on – and will be linked with presentations about these people skills.

The value of role plays, if they are conducted carefully and simulated as closely as possible to real life, is that the learners can practise newly learned techniques in a safe environment and have feedback. The latter is rare in real life, but is essential to let the learner know how well they are succeeding. The environment of the session in the training course is safe and, apart from giving the learners confidence, also allows them to experiment with techniques or approaches, experiments that would be dangerous in the real-life interview.

ACTIVITIES

The favourite and much-used supplements to the input session of many presenters are *activities* in their many forms. These, as with case studies and simulations, can be group activities or exercises in which the learners practise as a group the techniques related to the session with which they are linked. The participants are required to solve problems, demonstrate behaviours that can be observed and for which feedback can be given, and can practise the various forms of activity observation and subsequent feedback; and so on.

They can be job-related and linked with the subject of the session, but in many cases are non-job-related tasks – for example the construction of a jigsaw puzzle, the building of a mast or bridge with assorted material, the production of four-letter words from a base word. The tasks can be simple (like some of those above) or can be complicated, requiring not only problem-solving skills, effective behaviours and the use of leadership and group membership skills, but also creative and practical skills.

The extent and the complexity of the activities are constrained only by the time they need, the resources required and the creativity of the designer, but perhaps more than in most aspects of session design the designers must be careful not to let their enthusiasm for activities run away with them. If new techniques are being presented the presentation should be followed or accompanied by an activity – this doubles, *at least*, the time needed. Adding time for the review and feedback of the activity and the summary of the lessons learned: equals an exercise expensive in time.

VIDEOS

In addition to being used in other parts of a training programme, videos can be included in a presentation session to support that session. Most videos have duration of from 15 minutes to about an hour, the majority of 20–30 minutes, consequently their inclusion in a session does not in itself add too much time, although in some cases an additional 20 minutes may be too much. Care must also be taken to ensure the inclusion of time for review and discussion of the video – this can be substantial.

COMPUTER-ASSISTED TRAINING (CAT)

Computer programs can be included in presentation sessions in exactly the same way as described above for videos. The inclusion of a computer program, its nature and its timing will depend on the nature of the training and development session itself.

SOME ACTIVITIES TO CONSIDER

ACTIVITY: Consider and list the key situations in which you feel that adults are more likely to learn. Discuss these within your group and reach conclusions for presentation to the full group.

ACTIVITY

1.   Taking into account the types of audiences that you have spoken to or are likely to have to address, write down the list of situations identified in the Activity above and show at least two ways for each item of how you would satisfy these needs.
2.   As a potential audience member, consider how *you* would react to these solutions.

ACTIVITY: Consider, identify and list the ways in which the five senses – sound, sight, touch, taste and smell – might be used in various types of presentation. Bring this list back to the full group for amalgamation and production of a comprehensive statement.

ACTIVITY: Consider and discuss within your group the strategies you use to aid personal recall, and suggest other possible methods that you might use to improve your recall of information. Be prepared to discuss these on return to the full group.

ACTIVITY: Think about the memory trigger mechanisms of which you are aware and which work for you. Have you heard of any others or do your colleagues use mechanisms that you have either tried, but found do not work for you, or have not encountered previously? If so, get them to tell you about them and try them out yourself.

ACTIVITY: Consider first as an individual then in discussion with the others in your group:

■ Any recent presentations you have made and compare the techniques and methods you used with those described here.
■ Were you aware of any problems occurring? How did you become aware?
■ Did you use the most effective techniques and approaches? How do you know?
■ Which other forms of effective communication could you have used?
■ What are you going to do about your next presentation?

ACTIVITY

1. Consider your recent presentations and identify what action you took to analyze the audience before your presentation. If you made no analysis, why did you not do this and what steps could you have taken? If you made some analysis, was it sufficient? Could you have taken the analysis further with beneficial results?
2. Share your considerations and conclusions with the others in your group.

ACTIVITY

1. Consider a number of different types of topics – three or four should be sufficient – that could be the subjects of presentations. Preferably choose subjects that you may be required to present at some time in the future or ones about which you have substantial knowledge.
2. Summarize the main headings of the material that would form the content of these presentations and identify these in terms of Must, Should, and Could Knows.

ACTIVITY: Consider a presentation in whose design you were involved.

■ How did you go about it?
■ Which aspects went well? Why?
■ Which aspects did not go so well? Why?
■ What would you do again next time?
■ What would you change next time?

ACTIVITY

1. Consider a number of different types of topics – three or four should be sufficient – that could be the subjects of presentations. Preferably choose subjects that you may be required to present at some time in the future or ones about which you have substantial knowledge. You can also vary the types of audience.
2. Decide for each 'presentation' which type of approach might be the most appropriate.

3. Discuss your selections with the remainder of the group and be prepared to 'defend' your reasons for each approach.

ACTIVITY

1. Discuss within your group the subject of 'power' in a presentation; how you might react; how your usual audiences might react; what views your organization might have on the subject; and whether raising this subject introduces any moral issues of which a presenter should be aware.
2. List the results of your discussion and be prepared to present them to the full group.

3

Planning the Presentation – 2

The material in this chapter:

■ continues the planning process for the presentation and considers what actions you can take following consideration of your options
■ describes the methods of preparing for the presentation, including the preparation of scripts and briefs.

APPROPRIATE APPROACHES FOR THE SESSION

Once you know what needs to be included, what you would like to include and what you will have time to include, you can decide on the most appropriate and effective session approach. Reference back to Chapter 2, the material in this chapter, and more advanced sources should suggest this approach. You will then need to gather together all the material relevant to that approach and plan your session around it. Figure 3.1 summarizes these approaches and strategies, in terms of the type of strategy, its objectives – knowledge (**K**), skills (**S**) or attitudes (**A**), and the most important areas of effectiveness. Two asterisks are used to suggest activities that are most suitable to be included with presentation sessions (a single asterisk is given when their use is not a significant one).

Learning Experience	Objective	Areas of Effectiveness
Brainstorming: wide-ranging discussion to obtain ideas for solutions.	K, A, S	Creativity. New ideas. Problem-solving. Decision-making.
Buzz groups: groups of 2–6 people who discuss a matter for a short time without leaving the training room.	K, A	Encourages reticent people. Eases feedback.
Case studies: real or manufactured complex problems analysed in detail for solutions.	K, A, S	Encourage application of principles. Group working. Alternative points of view.
Controlled discussion: subjects are discussed under general control of the presenter.	K, A, S	Promotes understanding. Allows expression of points of view. How to use discussion. Behaviour identification.
Demonstrations: presenter, guest expert or member of group performs an operation or a skill while learners watch.	K, S	Practical skill training using real objects to show the elements of the operation.
Instructional talk/Input session: a talk (with visual aids, discussion, activity, handouts, etc) to present information, knowledge and details..	K, S	The basic strategy in a training event.
Lecture: an uninterrupted talk by the presenter, usually for larger audiences.	K	Provides information.
Question and answer: a series of questions from the presenter to the learning group.	K	To check understanding and encourage thought at all levels.
Practicals: an activity in which the learners carry out a task or process.	K, A, S	During or following an input to reinforce learning and practise skills and attitudes.

Figure 3.1 *Summary of training approaches and strategies*

Programmed learning: a text with a series of questions or tasks which must be completed before continuing to next stage. — K, S — Individual learning situations. Mixed pace groups.

Projects: an exercise in gathering information, performing a task or producing materials. — K, S, A — To consolidate and extend learning and encourage activity.

Reading: from a book, article or handout, in the training situation or away from it. — K — To prepare for learning, to reinforce other forms of learning.

**Role plays: learners are given roles, real or artificial, in a group or one to one, to carry out realistically or dramatically. — K, S, A — Reinforcing skills. Practising situations. Self-awareness. Attitude change.

Seminars: in one definition, a group of related topics — K — Encourage critical discussion on the series of topics. Group discussion. Presentations.

**Simulations: the duplication of a real situation as a complex problem or game with the learners taking on roles or positions. — K, S, A — Simulation of an activity which cannot be practised directly. Problem-solving. Team building.

**Syndicates – (or group working): learners formed into small groups and given identical or similar tasks to perform. Views or results are presented as from the group. — K, S, A — Problem-solving and decision-making in groups. Group behaviour. Leadership.

**Videos: the viewing by the learners of a pre-prepared video (commercial or internally produced) followed by discussion and review. — K — To reinforce learning, change the pace, insert variety.

SELECTING THE APPROPRIATE APPROACH

A knowledge of the approaches available for possible use in the presentation is essential, but is not the final step. With this knowledge, the most appropriate method for the presentation can be selected, this decision being recorded in the presentation plan. Figure 3.2 summarizes the factors that need to be taken into account.

The Content	**The Audience**
Knowledge	Learning styles (known?)
Skills	Knowledge of the subject
Attitude	Experience of the subject
Behavioural	Numbers
Technical	Needs identified
Operational	Common or diverse needs
General	Their expectations
Other specifics	Status of organizational level (relevant?)
The Organization	**Available Resources**
Organizational expectations	Your experience of the subject
Preferred methods	Your knowledge of the subject
Directives	
Traditional attitudes	Other presenter support
Progressive attitudes	Aids availability
Demands on presenter (dress, appearance, manner, attitude)	Time available
	Preparation time available and used
Evaluation requirements	Environmental factors

Figure 3.2 *Factors involved in selecting the appropriate approach*

SEQUENCING SESSION MATERIAL

Following the selection of the type of methods that should be included in a session (taking into account their relevancy to the subject and the time required), the next stage is to determine the general sequence in which the material should be presented. Obviously some of this sequencing will depend on the type of material and its complexity, but most sessions follow a series of classical sequences, summarized here.

- Known to the unknown
- Simple to complex
- Easy to difficult
- Logical stepping in a process
- Interesting material to more serious needs
- Random sequencing
- Dependency
- Knowledge to doing
- Doing to knowledge to doing

- **Known to the unknown**, the initial introduction of known material easing the learners into the situation and giving them confidence to progress.
- **Simple to complex** – it is usually a recipe for failure if at the start of a learning programme the learners are given a mass of highly complex material to learn before they have settled down, accepted the situation and are prepared to learn.
- **Easy to difficult** – for the same reasons mentioned above.
- **Logical stepping in a process** – care must, however, be taken to take into account the simple–complex, easy–difficult sequencing considerations.
- **Interesting material to more serious needs** – the sequences naturally suggested might need to be somewhat amended in order to introduce at the start material that will attract the interest of the learners so that they will be prepared to continue to learn. This will need to be taken into account when designing a programme of very 'heavy' or complex material.
- **Random sequencing** – some subjects might not require any logical or other sequencing, permitting planning that might depend on the availability of particular presenters or guest expert speakers, the length of time required for the various sessions to ensure that the material is contained effectively, etc.
- **Dependency** – some training, particularly in skill aspects of operational tasks, in spite of other considerations, requires the pattern of sessions to rely on the progression of learning. One danger in this approach of which the designer must be aware is that sequencing by this method is dependent on the slowest learner

– movement cannot be achieved until this slowest learner has understood the preceding material. One approach for avoiding this potential problem is to build into the programme the opportunity for these slower learners to have accelerated learning to the norm point by individual, special learning techniques.

■ **Knowledge to doing** – this approach can be amalgamated with other forms of sequencing as it involves ensuring that the learners are given the knowledge that allows them to perform the skill, eg by means of a practice activity. This approach is particularly useful when it is known that the learners have no previous knowledge of the material involved.

■ **Doing to knowledge to doing** – this approach reverses the previous method and uses a practical activity to initiate the learning process. The learners would be given a practical activity to perform, one that contains the learning points for that particular part of the programme, but not so complex that the activity cannot be performed at all. The errors or failures would be identified and their significance for the learning group assessed and discussed. This will be followed by a presentation of skill knowledge, models or theories, then further practice to confirm that the learning had been achieved. This approach can be particularly useful where the learners are known to have some previous knowledge or experience.

Training and development programmes are not (or should not be) written on stone as fixed and inflexible plans. So many factors can exist about which the designer, or even the presenter until the session is under way, will or can know nothing. The range of knowledge and skill level of individual learners has been mentioned several times and this factor can have an important effect on the progress of the session. The design must not be so set that it cannot be modified on the spot by the presenter because of such factors, otherwise the remainder of the session could fail. Individual sessions should link in a logical sequence with preceding and following ones, and should be capable of omission if circumstances at the time demand this.

By this stage the presenter has made most of the design and practice choices available and is ready to bring these together to formulate in formal terms the presentation or session that is to take place. The subsequent steps are detailed in the following material.

A DESIGN BLUEPRINT

Blueprints are normally associated with guiding producers of objects: a 'blueprint' can be produced similarly for the session and gives the 'big picture' for the presenters, in addition to giving the designer self-assurance that everything has been considered.

A written session blueprint should contain the following.

---

1. A statement of the aims and objectives of the session, stated in measurable terms, supplemented by information about timings.
2. Any information available about the potential or specific learning population, their likely existing knowledge and skills, and differences in status and organizational level that may have some effect on the practice of the session.
3. A checklist of the types of training methods to be included so that the relevant presenters can ensure that they are skilled in these methods.
4. Comments on the flexibility that will be allowed in the session for the use of more appropriate training methods.
5. Agreement that reviews with all designers and trainers or presenters concerned should be held following the first conducted event to consider its success or otherwise and any validation information obtained.
6. A note to discuss the agreed arrangements with the relevant administration section, in particular describing the requirements the session will place on this department.

THE SESSION GUIDE

By this point in the design and planning of your sessions you will have a firm idea of the objectives for the session, the content, the priorities for the various parts, the rough order of the material to be presented, and some initial views on the training aids you would like to use. Following on from the 'blueprint' many presenters find it useful to produce a session guide giving as much detail as possible about what will be included and how it will be presented, etc. The guide can be referred to when the session scripts and briefs are being constructed to ensure that everything necessary is included. At this stage the detail of the parts will not be included, only the general approaches, for example:

- input session including two buzz groups;
- more extended full group discussion;
- small group activity using problem-solving activity;
- review and feedback of activity, leading to
- summary of learning points emerging from the various stages of the session.

THE SESSION PLAN

The session plan follows on from the session guide and includes more detail. In many ways it can be considered as the initial part of the planning script (see below), but many trainers find it useful to look on it as a separate document on which the planning script is based. In addition to describing the proposed contents of the session, it can also include the stage directions that will need to be incorporated. The amount of detail will depend on the extent to which you already have detailed ideas of how your script will look, but the session plan should not become too detailed or reference to it will become too difficult and it may not be used. An example session plan is included in Figure 3.3.

THE PRESENTATION BRIEF

There are few presenters, whether or not they are experienced, who perform their presentation without any form of notes, script or brief. Inexperienced presenters are strongly advised to have this essential document, of whatever nature, always with them during their session.

Presentation briefs are also referred to as scripts or notes – I shall be referring to them as 'briefs', for a reason that will become obvious.

In a presenter's early days, it is certainly important for them to have prepared a full script of the presentation. But it is equally important that they do not use this to read from directly during the event. In fact, to have a full script immediately to hand is dangerous, as its presence might be a temptation to simply read it out, although full scripts have advantages:

- the material presented is guaranteed to be accurate and comprehensive within the construction of the presentation brief;
- reading the material will reduce the presenter's fear of forgetting what they should be saying.

SESSION PLAN FOR PRESENTATION SKILLS SESSION

		Approx time
I.	Introduce the session and describe the session objectives and methods. Seek information on group's experience of making presentations.	I0 minutes
2.	Give input session concentrating on skill attributes of session presentation. Include attention span and barriers to communication.	35 minutes
3.	During input, when communication barriers are to be introduced. Form buzz groups to identify possible barriers. Take feedback and display OHP slide as summary, adding group ideas.	(I2 minutes)
4.	Have learning group members present their ten minute sessions (previously arranged) – two groups of 4 = 4 x I0 minutes plus 4 x I0 minutes review of each presentation plus discontinuity time = 80 + 20 minutes	I hour 40 minutes
5.	Final review session	I5 minutes
Total session time		2 hours 40 minutes (allow 2 hours 45 minutes)

Figure 3.3 *A sample session plan*

There are, of course, also disadvantages:

- the learners might as well read the text themselves;
- written material read out usually sounds boring unless you are a skilled actor;
- eye contact would be lost with the group;
- non-verbal signals given by the group would not be noticed;
- the current place in the script could easily be lost if you were interrupted with questions, had to use a visual aid, or the flow of the reading was interrupted in some other way;
- astute members of the audience will start to identify how much more there is to the presentation from the number of sheets of paper remaining.

THE PRINCIPAL METHODS OF PRODUCING SCRIPTS OR BRIEFS

There are four principal methods.

1. The traditional, vertical method of planning and making notes
2. The headline method of producing a brief
3. The horizontal approach to planning and using a brief, including the 'pieces of paper' approach
4. Patterned notes.

THE TRADITIONAL, VERTICAL METHOD OF SESSION PLANNING

This is the full script method commented on above and, although it should not be used during the actual session, it has a valuable place when designing a session and writing the initial brief from which a working brief can be made.

Writing out text in full

In this case the text of the presentation is written out in full, word for word, as if it was a report or paper. However, the wording should be in the style of the 'spoken' word rather than the 'written' word. For example, in speaking we tend to say 'can't' rather than 'cannot' and so on.

The following guidance suggests helpful approaches to this technique.

Division into paras and sub-paras

It is helpful to divide the script into paragraphs and sub-paragraphs (each with their headlines), not for any grammatical or appearance reasons, but to make the different parts of the text clearer visually. Different colours can be used for alternate paragraphs (or sections) and if the brief is produced on a computer, different fonts can be used to aid this purpose.

Underlining for emphasis

One of the necessary steps to be taken with a script of this nature is to make the different parts as visually impactive as possible. Underlining, either <u>single</u> or <u>double</u> can be used, particularly **<u>with bold printing</u>** if this is available. Underlining is rarely used in printed books, the publishers appearing to favour italicizing the words, but judicious underlining in a script can be very helpful. However, as with any technique used to highlight parts of the brief, use the underlining sparingly or you will find that the impact is lost when too many parts are treated in this manner.

Colours for emphasis

Different colours can be used for producing emphasis in the document. These can be produced by the use of coloured pens if the script is handwritten, or coloured print if it is typewritten or word processed. In the latter cases, if monocolour only is available, colour can be added by using highlighter pens, and this highlighting can replace the need to underline.

Framing for emphasis or isolation

> Adding a frame or boxed border, particularly if combined with some or all of the previously described techniques, can be attention grabbing. Remember, however, that if too much use is made of this, as with any effect, the impact is lost.

Additional emphasis on the framing technique can be achieved by shading the box internally, or using white lettering on black shading.

> Adding a frame or boxed border, particularly if combined with some or all of the previously described techniques, can be attention grabbing, and shading can extend this emphasis. Remember, however, that if too much use is made of this, as with any effect, the impact is lost.

Adding a frame or boxed border, particularly if combined with some or all of the previously described techniques can be attention grabbing and lettering/shading reversal can extend this emphasis. Remember, however, that if too much use is made of this, as with any effect, the impact is lost.

Leaving broad margins

Broader than normal borders can be left on both sides of the text so that notes can be added – comments made during the session, amendments that become necessary as a result of these, directions to reconsider certain aspects and so on, in addition to stage directions such as those described in the next section.

Leave plenty of space between paragraphs or sections to isolate them or make the differences more apparent.

Stage directions

OHPs, handouts, questions, timings can all be added to the margins on each side of the text, or one margin only can be used to make stage direction entries such as:

- when to display which visual aid – OHP, flipchart, audio cassette, video and so on;
- when to issue a named or numbered handout;
- the point at which to ask a question;
- the occasion to break the group into sub-groups for an activity.

Timings can also be included at stages throughout the text. Do not write actual times – the session may not start at the advertised time and therefore any time will be wrong. Rather, enter the period of time by which the stage in the script should have been reached. If the session is divided into very definite sections, an alternative might be a time period for each section. However, if the timing of the presentation is inviolate, actual times can be used effectively.

HEADLINE PLANNING

This technique is a variation of the traditional full script method of preparing a brief and involves cutting out many of the words in the full script and using a shorthand form only. The method is as follows.

1. List headlines on A4 sheet

Identify the main subjects of the topic and list these as main subject headings, leaving space for relevant text below each heading. This order can initially be as the thoughts occur and, when all have been identified, a logical order can be produced by moving the headlines around. One initial source for this information might be a full written script – the headline brief can be the working brief developed from the full script.

2. Enter inter-heading summarized notes

Under each main subject heading (now placed in the logical order), enter brief, summary notes of the material. This will not be the final note, as the material will need to be edited for essential content.

3. Edit the rough script for final content

From the headings and summarized notes, which are now in the order for the presentation, edit the material using, for example, the Must, Should and Could Know approach until a final, headline and abbreviated text brief has been produced.

HORIZONTAL PLANNING

This method breaks away from the traditional approach by using the more natural, horizontal way that the mind works and produces a document, usually on one sheet of paper, which can be used both in the planning process and as a headline brief. The planning approach is in four stages.

Stage 1

The first decisions to be made are concerned with the main subject areas for the presentation. When the first thoughts on these are considered, they should be entered, preferably as single words, as column headings across a sheet of paper placed in the landscape position.

An example might be a presentation to a group of staff who are soon to move to another part of the country, relocating their homes and families. In such a case the column heading words could include:

TYPE OF HOUSE	AREA	TRANSPORT	SCHOOLS	SOCIAL AMENITIES	FINANCE	YOUNG PEOPLE'S JOB PROSPECTS	JOB PROSPECTS

These subject headings need not be complete, nor need they be in order, although this helps in the planning. Other headings may be added as the planning progresses and the final brief may appear in a completely different order from the one originally considered – it might be discovered in pre-presentation conversations that the group will have a strong interest in certain topics, some of which had not been afforded a high priority.

Stage 2

The second stage involves considering each subject heading and noting beneath it summary words or phrases describing the aspects relating to that subject. In the example used, under the heading TYPE OF HOUSE might appear the entries: Detached, semi-detached, town house, bungalow, cottage; 2, 3, 4 or more bedrooms; large, medium, small or no garden; garage, conservatory etc.

Sub-headings continue to be added until no more can be thought of – others can be added later if necessary. The sub-headings can then be considered for their prioritization and arranged into the order in which they would be discussed during the session.

Figure 3.4 illustrates the final form of a brief planned and presented in the horizontal planning format.

Stage 3

The final planning stage is concerned with adding the stage directions. If OHP slides are to be used or handouts issued, a note can be made to this effect alongside the relevant item.

Priority inclusions can be annotated. Session material can be considered at three priority levels – Must Know, Should Know and Could Know. To save space when entering them on the plan, these can be abbreviated to M, S and C.

HORIZONTAL PLAN FOR STAFF RESETTLEMENT IN ANOTHER AREA

TYPE OF HOUSE	AREA	TRANSPORT	SCHOOLS	SOCIAL AMENITIES	FINANCE	YOUNG PEOPLE'S JOB PROSPECTS	OTHER
Detached	In town	Private car	Nursery	Cinemas	Mortgages	Locally	Determine by
Semi-detached	Suburban	Sharing car	Infant	Theatres	Bridging loans	Travel-to-work area	audience analysis
Town house	Edge of	Taxi	Junior	Amateur drama	Relocation	Unemployment rate	and questioning
Bungalow	town	Motor bike	Secondary	groups	expenses	Job club support	what other
Cottage	In country	Bicycle	Comprehensive	Clubs or night	Transfer	Part-time jobs	information is
Number of bedrooms	Isolated	Walking	Grammar	clubs	grants	Vacation jobs	required
Large, medium, small	Housing estate	Rail or bus	Preparatory	Bingo halls	Removal		
or no garden	Near new work	Distance to	Private	Golf courses	expenses		
Garage, conservatory	Far from	station	Religion based	Libraries	House sale		
Old or new	new work	or bus stop	Buses	Youth clubs	support		
Good order or			Other travel	Leisure centres	Bank loans		
wanting renovation							
Private house:							
for purchase							
for renting							
Council house							

Figure 3.4 *A horizontal plan layout*

Linked with the prioritization can be estimates of the timing, at this stage for the main sections. More detailed timing can be included in the working brief.

The variety of detail possible in horizontal plans is great – colours can be used for emphasis; certain important items can be enclosed in a frame or block; different sized lettering can be used, lines with arrows can be added to show how items need to be moved for the final version or linking references made, and so on. Remember that this brief is your personal working document, so it should use all the aids that you find particularly helpful.

Stage 4

Finally, a fair copy of the plan can be used to produce a more traditional script and brief, or can be used as it stands. If used as the actual brief the stage directions may need to be supplemented or clarified.

Of course, as only headlines are included, the presenter must be fully aware of what needs to be said about each item, but the format has the decided advantage that the brief for one session can be contained on one, or at the most two sheets of paper. This is most helpful when locating the required place in the brief during a session. It also offers the advantage that, at a glance, the remaining material can be seen, or the order can be changed without moving pages about.

THE 'PIECES OF PAPER' APPROACH

Many people prefer this approach rather than working with a single sheet of paper.

The main subject headings mentioned above are written on small, rectangular pieces of paper – my own preference is to do this with a red pen. These pieces of paper are then spread out in a horizontal row on a table or on the floor – not necessarily in what will be the final order. On further pieces of paper are written – in a different colour ink – the sub-headings of the proposed content. These are then allocated as vertical rows to the main subject headings.

This obviously does not necessarily represent the final order of the presentation, but it is an easy task to move the pieces of paper around as required, rather than the more difficult procedure necessary in the sheet of paper approach.

The finally arranged structure will then need to be transferred to a working brief of the preferred type.

THE PATTERNED-NOTE METHOD

The patterned-note method was pioneered by Tony Buzan and, although originally proposed for taking notes, can be used in designing a presentation and preparing the session notes. This approach has a number of advantages once you become accustomed to working with it, but is not as easy to come to terms with as the other methods.

At the planning stage, the central box contains the key word for the session being designed. The first branches emanating from this box are annotated with the key words or phrases relating to the main subject areas. Again, at this stage in the design process these need not be in order round the centre, as the first pattern is usually only an initial working document. Sub-ideas are then added to the main branches to which they relate.

Colours, boxes, symbols (eg ?, *, ➜, ◆------➜, ☺, 📄, 🖥, +), directions – 'OHP', 'Issue h/o' etc, topic linking lines and so on can be added, particularly in different colours in order to make them stand out.

Once the initial pattern has been completed, the branches and their additions can be moved to their appropriate parts of the pattern, ie the order in which the subjects will be presented.

Figure 3.5 illustrates a simple patterned note. I find that when I am constructing a pattern single words are not sufficient for me; I need a phrase or sentence to remind me of the particular concept being recorded. But a patterned note is a very personal production, one which can often be understood only by the person who produced it. If necessary, therefore, the notes from the pattern can be converted to one of the more traditional formats. But when you become accustomed to patterned notes they can be used as the briefs for presentations.

One principal advantage, certainly as far as the session design pattern is concerned, is that it is contained on one sheet of paper – if the subject is complex a sheet of A3 could be used rather than the more usual A4. As a result the whole session can be seen at a glance without having to refer to a number of pages. This advantage can be extended to using the patterned note as the session brief itself, although this is a rather more difficult operation. Critical stages, links with other parts of the session, the material still to be covered and so on can all be seen at a glance, and script pages cannot slip out of order.

TRANSFER TO A WORKING BRIEF

The next stage is to transfer the design working documents into a working brief for use during the presentation. Some of the design

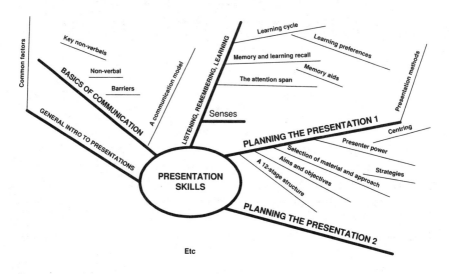

Figure 3.5 *A simple patterned note*

approaches already discussed may have already produced this, but others will need further action.

The purpose of producing a design for a session is so that you can use it as the basis for the actual presentation. As suggested above, your design document, when it has been ordered and annotated as required, can be used directly as your session brief. Or, when the notes have been completed – main subject headings and the contents of each section – you can transfer these notes to the format you will be using in the session itself. This might be sheets of A4 paper or index cards. The A4 sheets, which would normally rest on your desk or table, should be written in large enough print (not script) to be seen when you are standing beside the table as well as when you are seated.

Index cards can be completed with rather smaller print as you will normally hold these in your hand, but the print must still be sufficiently clear and large to be easily read from, for example, a standing position near the table.

COMPLETING A WORKING BRIEF

A working brief, whether on A4 sheets or index cards, will be difficult to use if all the entries are the same. As suggested in the design stage, full use of mixed print (upper and lower case), colour, underlining, boxes, highlighting, marginal stage directions and so on should be made. Err on the side of too few rather than too many as the latter can confuse, especially when you are quickly trying to find your place in the middle of a session.

NUMBERING AND TAGGING EACH SHEET OR CARD

Ensure that page numbers are entered on each sheet or card and punch a hole in the top left-hand corner of the sheet or card so that a tag can be inserted, holding the sheets together. It is all too easy to drop the set in the middle of a session with disastrous consequences if the sheets are not held together.

There is no golden rule about where the brief should rest during the session. Both paper sheets or index cards can be carried in the hand, or placed on your table. The former tends to make them more obvious to the audience, but if you need your brief to hand this can be ignored in favour of ensuring that you are able to make your session run freely. Much will depend on whether you are seated during the session, standing and walking about, or a mixture of both. My own method is to have the brief on the side of a small table in front of the group, and as I move about, if I have to refer to the notes I can (hopefully naturally) move over to the table and glance down at the notes.

Most new presenters say that they feel self-conscious about using notes and briefs in front of a group. In fact, usually the use of the notes is not as obtrusive as you think and, as stated above, it is better to ensure an effective and flowing session, even if the audience sees you using the notes, than to flounder and fail because you do not want to be seen referring to them.

PREPARATION TIME

However the circumstances for your presentation arise, it is essential that you have sufficient time to prepare. Of course, there will be occasions when this is not possible, but on those occasions when it appears that you are being pressed, it is always worth trying to negotiate some extra time.

Presentations take time to plan and prepare. How much you will need will depend on the complexity of the presentation, but generally at least seven to eight hours will be required for an hour's presentation. This will certainly be the case if you are a new or inexperienced presenter, and even more time is required if you intend using presentation aids, but even experienced presenters need a substantial amount of preparation time if the event is to be effective.

SOME ACTIVITIES TO CONSIDER

ACTIVITY

1. Consider a number of topics that could be the subjects of short presentations. Choose subjects that you may be required to present at sometime in the future or ones about which you have substantial knowledge.
2. Select a topic from this list, and prepare a planning brief and a working brief, using:
   (a) method that you have used previously; and
   (b) method with which you were previously unfamiliar.
3. Consider both briefs and try to assess their relative values, bearing in mind that the second one is one with which you are not familiar.

ACTIVITY

1. Consider and list the questions you should be asking yourself to determine the approach and style to be used in your presentations, taking into account the possible needs and attitudes of the potential audience.
2. Discuss your list with the remainder of your group and come to group conclusions about these questions. Be prepared to present the group's findings to the full group.

ACTIVITY

1. Identify the advantages and disadvantages of reading the script out in full at the presentation.
2. Identify and list any alternative forms of brief of which you are aware.
3. Discuss your findings with the remainder of your group and identify the advantages you see for the various forms.

ACTIVITY

1. Identify the ways in which the traditional, vertical form of planning script could be improved to make it more useful as a reference document. You will find it useful to use one of your previous briefs for this purpose if you have a suitable one available.
2. List your suggestions and compare them with the suggestions made during the session.

4

—

Preparing for the Presentation

The material in this chapter:

- identifies what action to take, as the presenter, both some time before and immediately before the presentation
- offers guidelines to help you ensure that you have done everything necessary to achieve a successful presentation.

PRE-EVENT INFORMATION AND TASKS

It should go without saying that as soon as the potential audience for a presentation or training session is known, they should be contacted and given as much information as possible about the event. Unfortunately this does not always happen. All too frequently potential participants are simply told the subject title, often by a third party. A rare occurrence, although it still happens, is for the individual to be informed that they are to attend at x time, at y place for a presentation or training session.

As a result of either of these two incidents, the participants arrive with feelings of:

- suspicion
- unease
- fear
- aggression
- no desire to accept the material or to learn.

None of these help the presenter to achieve effectiveness and can in fact make the presentation less than a success.

A solution to these problems would include sending the following to the participants (perhaps via their line managers).

---

1. A notification of the date, starting time, duration and location of the event
2. Where relevant, a map showing clearly the location and the methods of reaching it
3. The name(s) of the presenter or trainer(s)
4. A contact name for queries
5. A detailed copy of the programme, including its aims and objectives
6. The suggestion that participants should consider their own objectives and discuss these prior to the event with their line manager at the pre-course discussion, with the invitation to forward these objectives or any other problems to the named contact before the event
7. Where relevant and necessary, a request to individuals to perform some pre-event task or provide some information and, if appropriate, send the completed task or response to a named person, at a named location by a specific date
8. The request for immediate notification if individuals are unable to attend.

Most of these checklist guidelines are self-explanatory and many organizations have a standardized form and procedure. But the presenter must ensure that they have been carried out – otherwise there will be a knock-on effect on the efficiency and effectiveness of the event. Some of the items warrant further comments to help encourage their performance:

Item 5. Ensuring that intending participants have a copy of the aims and objectives for the event will act as their check on whether the event is the right one for them to attend. This will avoid people attending events that will not help them in their development, whether the event is a straightforward presentation or part of a skills training session.

Item 6. Discussing their aims and objectives with their line manager at a pre-event discussion will help to set a pattern for holding these pre-event discussions involving the line manager more than would otherwise occur. If the individuals send information about their objectives prior to the event to the presenter or trainer they will know whether the intended content is fully relevant, whether additional material needs to be included, and be aware of the existing level of potential participants.

Item 7. It has been suggested several times that there is considerable value in having as much information as possible about the participants before the event, particularly in terms of their existing experience and knowledge. This serves a twofold purpose: warning the presenters of this existing knowledge and skill and, where a full evaluation is to take place, establishing, for example, the pre-training level that can eventually be compared with the post-training level.

It is essential that, if information or other responses have to be sent prior to the event, full details of how this should be done are clearly stated. Too often the instruction is left at 'when you have completed x, you should send the results to y'. This is leaving the way open for the material to arrive too close to the event, or even brought with a participant – and this is not infrequent. Give clear indications of to whom it should be sent, where, and by when. If you are to receive half of the material too late, or not receive some at all, in many cases it would have been better not to have made the request in the first place. A useful ploy is to enlist the help of the line manager in ensuring prompt return.

PRE-EVENT TASKS OR TESTS

The value of these has been commented on earlier and they form a significant and important part of any material on the evaluation of training and other events. Unfortunately too often the potential value of these pre-event contacts is lost by failure to follow a set of simple rules. These include:

- Send the material in ample time
- Is this pre-event work available?
- Has the material been received?
- Experiment extensively to assess completion times
- Make the material neither too difficult nor too easy
- Require specific information from reading material
- Use any requested pre-event task material
- Ask for real work examples to be brought
- Print pre-event material on a different coloured paper

- Send the material in ample time before the event. If the potential participant has to do some pre-event reading, how long does this take (remember slow readers)? If it involves a project or work-related task, is this work available where the individual is located?

- Ensure that you know that the material has been received. Include a reply slip, or require some other immediate confirmation that the material has been received.
- Experiment extensively when designing pre-event materials so that the maximum, average and minimum times for their completion is known and can be quoted to the individual.
- Do not make the material too difficult or complex as this may frighten the individual about the event and may even cause them to cancel. On the other hand, making it too simple may ensure that everyone completes it successfully, and that will tell you nothing. Balance the 'tests' so that something can be achieved, but the remainder will test the actual knowledge of what the event will be about.
- Some pre-event work might suggest reading handouts or books – this is usually found to be the least successful of all pre-event tasks. The material is either not read or, if it is, so superficially as to have no effect. Rather, require the readers to seek out certain, specific information from the material and use that as their pre-event response.
- Successful performance of pre-event tasks should ensure that all participants are at about the same level of skill or knowledge when they attend – this makes the presenter's task so much easier.
- Make sure, if you ask the people to perform some pre-event task, that when they eventually attend you either use this material or at least refer to it in a significant way. Otherwise, next time you ask them (or a colleague to whom they have complained) you are less likely to achieve success.
- If you are going to ask them to perform work-related tasks during the event ask them to bring real work examples of these along with them to use. This not only ensures practical work application but also lets them know that the event is going to have pragmatic aims.
- A simple guideline, but one that both you and the participants will find useful – any pre-event material should be printed on a different coloured paper to that used during the event.

USING EXTERNAL GUEST OR EXPERT SPEAKERS

Guidelines for using external guests or expert speakers are summarized opposite.

- Make sure that they *really are* experts
- Where possible invite guests who are also capable speakers
- Offer some tuition in presentation skills if necessary
- Inform them in writing of the aims and objectives of the session
- Confirm what you want them to cover; how long they have to speak; and what questioning technique will be employed
- Give information, in writing, about starting time, location, size and level of audience
- Will they use aids?
- Are any of the advanced aids you have available wanted?
- Is there a need for any particular type of aid equipment?
- Are they going to use handouts?
- What are their views on room layout?
- Confirm your role during their contribution
- Arrange a feedback session
- Send a 'thank you' letter soon after the event

It is quite common to invite a guest speaker who may be an expert in a particular aspect of the subject to take part in the presentation or other event. This is an area fraught with difficulties, but many can be avoided by following some simple rules.

- Before inviting the guest, make sure that they *really are* experts in the relevant subject.
- Invite, if possible, guests who are not only experts in the subject but are also capable speakers.
- If, although they are eminently suitable because of their expertise, they have poor presentation skills, offer them some tuition.
- Inform them in writing, and in clear and unambiguous terms, of the aims and objectives of the session or other event in which they will be participating.
- Discuss with them then confirm in writing specifically what you want them to cover; exactly how long they have to speak; and what questioning technique will be employed – during or after their contribution.
- Give them full information, in writing, about the starting time, the location, and the size and level of the audience.
- Confirm whether they will use aids and, if so, of what type(s) and how many. Do they already have them; are they of acceptable quality; do they want any help in producing them; do they want to use any of the advanced aids you have available?

- Confirm whether they want or would prefer any particular type of aid equipment.
- Confirm whether they intend to use handouts: do they have them available; do they want any support in their production; when do they intend to use them?
- Seek and confirm their views on room layout – what type they would prefer or whether they have to accept the existing room layout.
- Confirm whether they want you to be a passive observer during their part of the session or whether you could or should intervene.
- Arrange a feedback session with the guest presenter – you may want to use them again.
- Send a 'thank you' letter soon after the event.

PREPARING THE ENVIRONMENT

There are times when the presenter has the 'luxury' of being able to modify the environment in which the presentation is to be given. Grasp this opportunity with both hands, as more often than not you will be presented with a situation determined by the programme organizers, the conference centre or hotel, or simply by the nature of the room in which you have to perform. Even in these latter cases there are actions that (a) you must do and (b) you should do if you can.

Preparation will fall into two stages, the first being well in advance of the presentation – usually soon after the arrangements are made for you to give the presentation; the second, less extensive, will be immediately before the actual presentation.

THE PRESENTATION ROOM

Although you may have little or no control over the physical attributes of the room in which you are to make your presentation, you should demand certain minimum standards. The ideal room for a presentation to a small audience or in a training environment should be as shown in Figure 4.1.

This layout is very effective for a variety of presentations when a small group of people, say 10–14, are involved. It is particularly useful in training or other presentations when a variety of audio and visual aids are to be used.

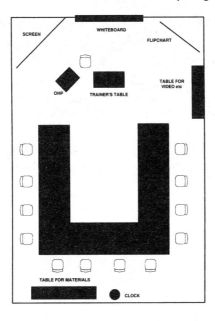

Figure 4.1 *The 'ideal' presentation room layout*

The advantages of this layout include:

■ The front wall can be fully utilized, particularly if there is a system of equipment tracks.

■ It is relatively simple to move from the presenter position to either the whiteboard or flipchart.

■ The 'U'-shaped seating affords reasonable visibility.

■ Tables can be placed in front of the seats, which can be easy chairs, or 'student-type' chairs with a flat arm on which to rest a notepad.

■ The presenter has good visibility of all the audience and can therefore maintain good eye contact, and is not behind a table or desk barrier (although one is near at hand for briefs, handouts and use as a video table when necessary).

■ The seating configuration can be easily altered to accommodate, for example, buzz groups or paired discussions.

■ The OHP is easily available.

■ The video can be kept out of the way and placed on the presenter's table when required.

■ The screen is easily visible from most of the audience positions.

■ The tables at the back of the room can be used for reference material, computer positions or as refreshment tables.

The room layout has to be rethought when the audience group is larger than this, the actual size often dictating the layout.

ENVIRONMENTAL AND ALLIED QUESTIONS TO ASK

There will be many occasions when the 'ideal' is not possible, when you are presented with a layout to which you can make only limited modifications, or the event – for example, when there is to be a very large audience – requires a different seating formation. You will need to take into account a number of factors: many of these can be determined by asking a series of questions.

- How large an audience will there be?
- How big is the room?
- To what extent is this size going to affect your vocal presentation? (How loudly am I going to have to speak to be heard at the back of the room?)
- What will the nature of the event be? (The amount of interactivity will have a major effect on the layout and audience intervisibility.)
- Will there be discussion?
- Which types of visual aids are going to be (a) possible (b) the most effective?
- Which aids are provided and are they satisfactory (modern, working) or do I need to take my own?
- Where am I going to place the visual aids equipment: flipchart, overhead projector, video monitor etc?
- Can the visual aids be seen by all of the audience?
- Where, how many and what type of power points are available?
- (In conjunction with the size of the audience) can I sit or stand?
- Will I be required to sit behind a desk or stand behind a lectern?
- Is there any opportunity to move these?
- Will I be using a brief, OHP transparencies, handouts?
- Will there be a suitable location to place these items?
- Are there alternative places to put (a) my brief (b) my OHP transparencies (c) my handouts?
- Will movement be impeded in any way?
- Will I be easily visible from all parts of the audience?
- What is the seating arrangement?
- Is this the most effective?
- Can it be modified in any way? Permanently? For a buzz group event etc?
- Is there a visible clock in the room?
- Where are the toilets?

These are some of the principal questions for which you need to obtain answers; I am sure others will occur to you – add these to the list.

SOME BARRIERS (AND BENEFITS) TO AN EFFECTIVE ENVIRONMENT

Room too large	May overpower a small audience
	May inhibit discussion/participation
	May prevent audience/speaker rapport and interrelationships
	Small audience may feel lost in the large space.
	(*Can accommodate a larger audience*)
	(*Maintains formality if required*)
Room too small	Audience might feel claustrophobic
	Personal space may be cramped
	Size of audience restricted
	(*Close audience/speaker relationship*)
Pillars in large room	Will restrict vision
Lighting	If too low/too high can disturb audience's comfort
	Too low light prevents notetaking
	Inhibits intervisibility if too low
Tables	Can be seen as barriers
	Barriers to movement
	Restrict placement of audience
	(*Can be used to place materials or on which to write*)
	(*May make individuals feel safer*)
Irrelevant decoration and posters	Give an unprofessional appearance
	Can interfere with attention
Glass doors, windows – external and internal	Movement visible outside the room can interfere with attention
Platform	Makes speaker remote from audience
	Reduces speaker/audience rapport
	(*Improves visibility of speaker*)
	(*Improves visibility of visual aids*)
	(*Speaker able to see more of audience more easily*)
Lectern	Acts as barrier between speaker and audience
	(*Stops too much movement by speaker*)
	(*Useful for speaker's notes etc*)
Intervisibility	(*Essential for certain types of events, not for others*)

POSSIBLE VARIATIONS OF LAYOUT

Presentation rooms can be arranged in a variety of ways, and the ideal arrangement will obviously depend on the circumstances – the type of room, the seating available, whether the seats are movable, the number of participants, the style of presentation and so on – and whether you can modify the existing layout. Some of the possible arrangements with their advantages and disadvantages are discussed here.

The theatre or classroom

Format

When numbers are large, the traditional seating arrangement for meetings is the theatre or classroom style, in which chairs are placed in rows one behind the other. The presenter is seated at a table at the front of the rows of seats, perhaps at a considerable distance from the furthest row.

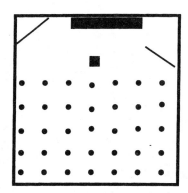

Advantages

- It is easy to set up.
- A large number of people can be accommodated.
- If it is possible to arrange, with small people avoiding sitting behind large people, the presenter is visible to most of the audience and the audience to the presenter.
- It is certainly suitable (or most suitable) for large audience groups.
- The layout is obviously a formal one, but the formality may be reduced with audiences below certain sizes.

Disadvantages

- Everybody is facing the front.
- If an interactive event is required, this becomes much more difficult – although not impossible.
- If any discussion takes place the various parts of the audience have limited views of the speakers.
- People at the back may have difficulty seeing and hearing.
- Visual aids need to be large – only some are suitable.
- The speaker and the audience may feel remote from each other.
- A presenter, even an experienced one, can be intimidated by the sea of faces.

The herringbone

Format

The rows of seats, instead of all being carefully arranged so that everybody looks straight forward because the rows are parallel to the front of the room, are in rows which are diagonally inclined. The outside of a row is nearer the front than the centre, thus producing an arrow shape pointing away from the front.

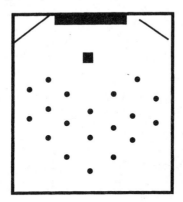

Advantages

- In addition to the advantages described for the traditional theatre layout, the staggered seating arrangement somewhat improves the visibility between members.

The boardroom

Format

This is the traditional arrangement for small- to medium-sized groups, in which the members sit round the outside of a large table or number of tables placed together, with the presenter at the 'head' of the table (a rectangular configuration will have two 'heads', but one will often be recognized as the presenter's seat). In many ways this layout can be compared with the U shape, the difference being that the base of the 'U' is usually longer and the presenter, at the head, is separated from the main table.

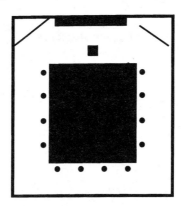

Advantages

- The presenter is visible, to a greater or lesser extent, to all the people seated round the table, and the audience is reasonably visible to the presenter.
- For numbers up to about 20, everybody is reasonably close to the presenter.
- The table provides a facility for holding papers etc.
- The table, with the audience on each side, can act as a barrier, suggesting greater security.
- The presentation usually has a formal atmosphere (if this is required).

Disadvantages

- Visibility between people seated along the same axis – for example, down one side of the table – is limited and can therefore inhibit discussion.
- When the numbers exceed about 20, the space taken up is large unless the individuals are crowded together.

- Some members can be quite remote from the speaker.
- There can be an atmosphere of confrontation with people sitting opposite each other, across the table, when they are much closer than in the U-shaped room layout.
- The table can be seen as an unnecessary barrier and can inhibit informality.
- People seated at the furthest points may have difficulty seeing and hearing.

The open boardroom

Format

The open boardroom seating arrangement is similar to the traditional boardroom, but instead of the table being solid, the constituent tables are moved outwards so that a well exists within the rectangle. Other audience members are able to sit in this well.

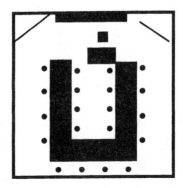

Advantages

- The size of the audience can be increased with only a small increase in floorspace.

Disadvantages

- The people sitting inside the well are sitting with their backs to others in the well and can only see the people on the other side of their table.

The cabaret, restaurant or cluster layout

Format

This is a more casual type of layout that uses small tables scattered unevenly around the room. In more formal presentations using this layout, the seats with their backs to the speaker can be omitted, although this does not stop the members moving round to fill the empty spaces! A space can be left at each table for presenters to place a chair and sit if they are observing a group during an activity.

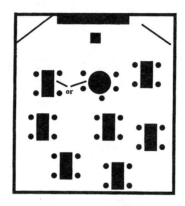

Advantages

- Introduces an informal tone into the presentation.
- Allows table groups to get to know each other.
- Affords irregular space for the presenter to move about around the tables.
- Useful for buzz groups and other small-group activities within the presentation.
- Allows some intervisibility between tables.
- Gives members something on which to write or rest materials.
- Location of tables is easily changed.

Disadvantages

- Some members will have to swivel round to look at the speaker.
- Interaction between distant tables is difficult.
- Unwanted, individual table discussions can occur.

The circle

Format

As the name suggests, the seats in this arrangement are placed in a circle facing towards the centre, the presenter being part of the circle. An alternative is to move the speaker's chair away from the circle, but this destroys the complete informality of the situation.

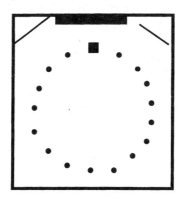

Advantages

- Encourages maximum informality.
- Encourages optimum participation in discussion.
- Minimum side discussions and mini-groupings.
- No physical barriers unless tables are also arranged in the circle.

Disadvantages

- Complete intervisibility is still not achieved, nearer neighbours not being able to see each other easily.
- Unless the circle is large, the chairs are in close proximity to each other.
- A large area is required to produce an effective circle.
- Difficulty of finding tables that can be placed easily in a circle. (If tables are not used the participants have nowhere on which to place papers etc.)
- Difficult to use visual and other aids.
- Some people may find it too informal.

The U-shape

Format

This is a layout in the shape of a 'U' which can be used with or without tables in front of the learners, their presence depending on whether there will be a lot of writing and reference to papers, or whether the activity will be mainly verbal and the presentation not always 'passive'. The base of the U can be either rounded or squared-off. If tables are used, the members sit round the outside of the tables, rather like the boardroom layout and, again like the boardroom, if more members have to be accommodated they can sit at the inner sides of the tables.

Advantages

- Tables are easy to arrange in this configuration.
- Most members can see each other easily, with the exception of the ones seated at the base of the 'U'
- All members are clearly visible to the speaker.
- The speaker can move readily into the 'U' if necessary.
- A standard layout and consequently non-threatening to the audience.
- Allows flexibility in the placing of visual aids.
- Promotes discussion and interrelationships.

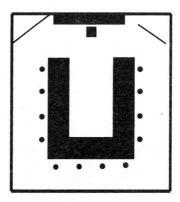

Disadvantages

- Can appear to be slightly formal, and might produce the audience reaction 'Oh no, not the horseshoe again!'
- Might encourage 'opposite sides' conflict or confrontation.
- If base of 'U' is broad, members seated there can have some difficulty in seeing each other.

- Care has to be taken in placement of visual aids for total visibility.
- If group is large, ends and base of 'U' may be a long way from speaker and visual aids.

The V-shape

Format

This is a natural development of the 'U' shape, in which the seats are arranged in the form of a 'V' rather than a 'U'.

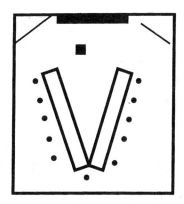

Advantages

- Less formal than the 'U' shape and consequently less intimidating.
- Less frequently used than the 'U' and so avoids the audience reaction of 'not again', but rather produces a positive reaction.
- Avoids poor intervisibility at part of layout furthest from speaker.
- Otherwise has all the advantages of the 'U' shape
- Avoids the 'across the table' attitude.

Disadvantages

- Difficult to place tables in the optimum shape.
- Need for speaker and visual aids to be located effectively, otherwise there will too much head twisting by some people.
- Requires much more space than the 'U' shape.
- Difficult for larger groups in terms both of space and seeing and hearing difficulties for people near the point of the 'V'.
- Some members may find difficulty in seeing all visual aids.

CHECKS TO MAKE IMMEDIATELY PRIOR TO THE PRESENTATION

Some arrangements, such as the environmental and allied questions asked earlier and those for the room layout will have been made at an early stage, but the wise presenter will have a checklist of items to confirm either shortly before the date of the presentation, or before the presentation itself. This may not always be easy or possible, especially if you are one of a series of speakers. If you are the first or only speaker, it is essential that you visit or arrive at the presentation location well before the allotted time to perform your checks and 'lay out your stall'. Some of the items to check are shown below.

- Do you have with you the relevant brief?
- Do you have with you all the visual aids?
- Is the relevant visual aid equipment available?
- Does it all work correctly?
- Is replacement equipment readily available if required?
- Is the seating layout as you required, or the best available?
- Can the visual aids be seen clearly by all the audience?
- Is there a clock easily visible to you? If not, you will have to take your own.
- If relevant, are tables provided and are there writing materials provided?
- Have the room temperature and ventilation arrangements been made and are they working?
- Are all the other room arrangements satisfactory?
- Do you know who to contact in case of problems and where they are to be found?
- Are the administration staff aware of the interruptions policy?
- Have refreshment arrangements been confirmed?
- Have any changes occurred since the original check?

A PRE-PRESENTATION CHECKLIST

This checklist is intended as a guide only. Omit any items which are not relevant to your needs and add any which are.

A pre-presentation checklist

Environment

Room booked

Syndicate or break-out rooms booked

Access method

Electrical sockets needed or available

Suitability of room for event

Other required rooms available

Parking facilities

Porterage access

Seating arrangements

Sufficient chairs, tables etc

Toilets locations and availability

Telephone access

Fax availability (if relevant)

Computer availability (if relevant)

Clerical or secretarial contact

Location or equipment contact

Lighting control

Wall space for posters etc

Ventilation regulation

Refreshment availability and arranged

Photocopier availability

Posters, screen shots visible

Equipment

Audio recorder and tapes

Video recorder, monitor and tapes

Video camera, camcorder, mixer, tapes

Directional signs as necessary

Extension cords

Microphones – needed, type, fitted

Overhead projector

Flipchart, stand and paper

Film projector and screen

Slide projector and screen

Lectern

Whiteboard and wiper

Materials

(It is useful to keep a box with the items marked * as an emergency toolkit.)

Nameplates

Blotter pads

*Small felt-tip pens or similar

*Large felt-tip pens or similar

*Drymarker pens

*Lumocolour pens – water and spirit based

*Highlighter pens

Acetate sheets and rolls

*Pencils

*Masking tape

*Blutack

*Paperclips

*Scissors

*Stapler

*Hole punch

Flipchart paper

*A4 lined/plain paper

File folders

Clipboard
Visual aids
Bottled water, juices etc
*Screwdrivers
*Extension cable and variable
    adapter

Reference books
Water carafes and glasses
Bowls of sweets etc
*Selection of fuses

Immediately before training event

Check all seating, tables,
    extra seating available
Check all other rooms available

Check equipment available and
    working

Check refreshments –
    water and other supplies
    available
Confirm guests coming
Clock available, working and
    correct
Room booked and available
Access method
Your visual aids
Spare copies of handouts etc
    available

Secretarial assistance available
Contact available

Other rooms booked and available
Your brief
Your handouts

If at all possible, before your presentation, visit the event location and answer the relevant questions. Never assume that the hotel or conference venue staff will automatically know how to prepare a room for a presentation, the type of layout you require, or will necessarily set up the room according to your request. A useful tip, when discussing layout with the location organizers, is to give them a diagram of the required layout. Finally, make your visit immediately prior to the presentation early enough to put something right if necessary.

A FINAL CHECK

■ If you are the only presenter, and can control this, make arrangements for light refreshments to be available before the presentation. There are always participants who arrive well before time and this can impress them and put them in the frame of mind to consider (although not necessarily accept) your presentation more readily.

- In addition to confirming the times for refreshments, make sure that the catering staff are aware of your requirements for clearing away the debris. If possible, have all refreshments served in a different room to the presentation.
- Ensure that the audience is aware of the smoking (or, more relevantly, non-smoking) restrictions and where and when any smokers can go to indulge.
- It is normal for any audience to start filling up seats from the rear, avoiding the first two or three rows. Put 'reserved' labels on the last two or three rows until the forward rows are filling up! An alternative (certain not to endear you to the audience), in the case of a smallish group and when everybody is seated is to ask them to turn their chairs through 180 degrees and make your presentation from the opposite end of the room!

A PRESENTER'S TOOLKIT

If you are scheduled to make a number of presentations especially if they are in different locations, you will find it useful to have a 'toolkit' that you can take with you on your travels, plus a short checklist of more personal items that you know you need. The following is a suggestion of what you might include, but you will obviously need to add your own items.

- Pad of paper, A5 or A4, according to what you normally use
- Blank index cards
- Pens, pencils, dry-marker pens, marker pens, Lumocolour pens (water based and permanent)
- Masking tape
- Blu-tack
- Stapler and box of staples, paperclips, post-it pad, scissors, ruler, erasers
- Calculator
- Diary and address list

Plus, as required

- Change of clothes – in addition to a normal change, have a spare shirt/blouse to change into during the day, and also your 'working clothes' into which you can change before the presentation if you have had a long drive in casual clothes
- Toiletry items

SOME ACTIVITIES TO CONSIDER

ACTIVITY: Discuss and compare with the other members of your group the processes you or your supporters follow to contact course members before their attendance. Discuss particularly any differences and their advantages or disadvantages in various situations.

ACTIVITY: Discuss and compare with the other members of your group and identify any failings in the tasks you set or any advantages in those set by others. Reach some conclusions about the most suitable pre-event task approach for: a knowledge course; a skills course; a people skills course; a behavioural event.

ACTIVITY: Identify the most effective actions to take when inviting and including a guest/expert speaker to an event you run or are to run.

ACTIVITY: Consider and discuss with your group three presentations you have attended (including training course input sessions).

(a)   Describe the physical environment and your views on its suitability or otherwise ˙
(b)   Did it contribute to the success of the presentation? How?
(c)   Did it detract from the presentation? How?
(d)   How could you have improved some of these events?

ACTIVITY: Consider different presentations you have attended and describe some of these to the remainder of the group. What effect did the environment of each of these events have on you, your learning, listening, receptivity etc.

ACTIVITY: Consider the training and development events you currently offer; describe the environment and determine (a) whether this is the most effective one for this event or (b) whether you could improve the environment in some way and thus improve the effectiveness of the event.

ACTIVITY: (This activity will be most effective if it follows a session on effective environments and the learning group has had a refreshment break.) During a break, rearrange the room and its contents so that as much as possible is inappropriately located. Invite the learning group to rearrange the room as effectively as possible within the environmental constraints. If the arrangement is different from the original, have the group justify their rearrangement.
  Seek views on the most appropriate arrangement if no environmental constraints existed and what, if anything, might be done to alleviate these.

ACTIVITY: A quasi-environmental activity can be linked with a relationship development exercise in certain situations. During a refreshment break soon after the start of the event while the learners are absent from the room, rearrange the seats into obvious but random groups of two, three and four, rearranging also the nameplates for the delegates. On their return to the room, ask them to sit in their new places. They can then be asked to try to identify the reasons why the room has been rearranged into the new groupings and memberships. Following the discussions in the small groupings, ask for and list the reasons suggested.

Following discussion, disclose the random actions and, if it has not already been suggested, comment on the value of the seating arrangement with its small groups. You should make a decision whether you will also disclose the sub-agenda of having the participants change their seating so that they could get to know other people – seek their views on this and participant reaction to apparent manipulation of this nature. (It may be that you have deliberately separated certain members for particular reasons but it is usually unwise to disclose this!)

5

—

Presentation Aids

This chapter:

■ describes the use of the more commonly used aids:

a particular object	the presenter
flipcharts	whiteboards
overhead projectors	video OHPs
audio equipment	computers
video	handouts

THE AIDS IN NORMAL USE

Few successful presentations rely on the presenter's verbal presentation alone. Most are supported by some form of presentational aid, usually a visual aid; this is the term in common use, whether or not the aid is visual alone. The range of these and other audiovisual aids now is wide, although most presenters are restricted to a few, basic ones.

The aids in normal use today are listed below, the two asterisks identify those most commonly used in presentations. These are described following the list; the production and use of all the audio and visual aids available are described in another recent publication (*Training Aids: A Complete Resource Kit for Training and Development,* Leslie Rae, Kogan Page, 1997).

```
**a particular object
*presenters themselves
**flipchart
**whiteboard
**overhead projector
audio cassette player and combined
    audio and slide presenter
*video
*computer
*slide projector
**handouts
```

A PARTICULAR OBJECT

Having the object itself physically present is the most effective aid to support many forms of presentation.

In some cases it will not be possible to have the object itself in the room – for example a large piece of equipment – nor to visit the site – a distant location – and so on. In such instances an alternative can be a photograph of the object, either passed round the audience or projected; a model; an OHP diagram; a computer graphic; an audio or video recording. The latter applies particularly where a sequence is involved (even home camcorders can be valuable for this purpose) and is a very powerful aid, as most people are accustomed to moving pictures and relate easily to the television screen.

The object as a visual aid requires little verbal description – objects speak for themselves and so make effective training aids. The presenter can demonstrate the use of, for example a computer, using the 'Tell, Show, Do' technique. In this approach the computer can be briefly described verbally as an instrument used to support the presenter as a visual aid mechanism; the computer and its software program can then be revealed and described in detail. Finally, the learners can be given the opportunity to handle it.

This approach can be used for many objects, although some will require careful handling both by the presenters and the audience.

THE PRESENTER AS A VISUAL AID

Although many presenters may not appreciate the fact, they are themselves one of their most powerful and visible visual aids, and can have considerable impact on the audience. If the aim of the presentation concerns motivation an obviously motivated and enthusiastic presenter will demonstrate to the audience that such an attitude is possible. If the event is concerned with the interactive skills of the culture, the presenter's own interactivity is a role model which the audience can be encouraged to take up. One of the most common examples of the use of this aid also links with the use of the object and can be seen every time you fly. At the start of the flight the cabin staff demonstrate – *on themselves* – the use of the lifejacket, seat belt and the location of the emergency exits.

Further consideration of the appearance etc of the presenter and its effects is given in Chapter 7.

FLIPCHARTS, WHITEBOARDS AND OVERHEAD PROJECTORS

Three frequently used aids are artificial objects and all have their advantages and disadvantages. The flipchart, a pad of fairly substantial A1 size paper, is the modern equivalent of the earlier 'newsprint', sheets of thin, brownish-toned paper of approximately A1 size. The whiteboard is a development from the flipchart and is the modern equivalent of the old chalkboard (or blackboard as it was more commonly called, even though it was often green!). The OHP is the electric, projection version of the flipchart or whiteboard. All three have fairly similar uses, the variations being the result of different requirements, environments and techniques. The advantages and disadvantages are summarized at the end of each section.

The flipchart

Advantages

- **Adaptable** – can be used either as a blank sheet to write on or as a prepared sheet, the contents of which can be disclosed in a variety of ways.
- **Any paper usable** – the 'flipchart paper' itself need not be commercially produced; any large sheet of paper can be used.
- **Easy to use** – few basic skills, other than clear writing, are required.

- **No power required** – unlike the OHP, slide projector, video etc, no power supply is required so you can carry on using it even during a power failure.
- **Easily displayed** – sheets of paper, even the A1 size of the normal flipchart, are relatively light and can be posted on walls, doors, cabinets, and even curtains, using a dry, reusable adhesive such as BluTack.
- **Retained for reference** – each sheet can be torn from the flipchart pad and retained as a poster.
- **Simple, cheap, needs little training** – a principal advantage. The necessary training is in how to write legibly on a flipchart, together with some techniques for creating impact and using the aid effectively.
- **Transportable** – the sheets of paper can be easily rolled up and the stand collapsed so that both can be relatively easily carried.
- **Ready for immediate recording** – no preparation is necessary if it is to be used as a large jotting pad during a presentation.

Disadvantages

- **Easily torn, dirtied and dog-eared** – although easily portable, it is also easy to damage the sheets in transit or in storage.
- **If badly prepared, can look unprofessional** – a poor appearance can be offputting to the audience and the presenter's credibility can be reduced.
- **Special techniques difficult** – covering cards held by BluTack or paper clips can be used for disclosure, or constant reference backwards and forwards to various sheets can be helped with folds and clips – both these techniques can easily go wrong.
- **Usually only of temporary value** – because paper is used, this aid has a limited life, which can reduce its value if it is important enough to be retained and reused.

ADVANTAGES	DISADVANTAGES
Adaptable	Easily torn, dirtied and dog-eared
Any paper usable	If badly prepared, can look unprofessional
Easy to use	Special techniques difficult
No power required	Usually only of temporary value
Easily displayed	
Retained for reference	
Simple, cheap, needs little training	
Transportable	
Ready for immediate recording	

The whiteboard

With the appropriate dry-marker pen you can write or draw on a whiteboard, which has many similarities with the flipchart. It is less portable, being usually much larger (although whiteboards from about 6 inches by 4 inches can be obtained), can be easel or wall mounted. Entries can be erased – this is both an advantage and a disadvantage: the board can be continuously used and reused, but unless you have more than one board material cannot be retained. Some advanced whiteboards have more than one 'board' which can be displayed electrically and others have a photocopying facility so that the material can be copied on to A4 paper – useful when an immediate handout is required.

ADVANTAGES	DISADVANTAGES
Can write or draw with dry-marker pen	Usually much larger
Entries can be erased	Less portable
Can be continuously used and re-used	Entries can be erased
Electronic whiteboards have more than one 'board'	
Some have a photocopying facility	

The overhead projector

Advantages

- **High visual impact** – because the image is projected by a light source, the visual impact can be high compared with a rather dull flipchart.
- **Large image** – the projected image can be large, the actual size limited only by the size of the screen or projection area, the light intensity of the projector and the type of lens used.
- **OHPs widely available** – this item of equipment is nowadays almost as freely available as the flipchart; if it is not available where required, portable models are easily transportable.
- **Professional production** – OHP slides can have a very professional appearance, whether they are made skilfully by hand, by commercial photographic techniques, or, more commonly now, from computer graphics.
- **Slides easily portable** – the acetate slides used with the OHP, whether or not mounted in card frames or in transparent folders, can be carried easily in a folder, briefcase or slide carrying case.

- **Usable in light** – unlike slide and film projectors, the room does not need to be darkened and so you have continuous eye contact with the learning group.
- **Used sitting or standing** – some presenters prefer to sit while presenting, others prefer to stand and/or walk about; the OHP permits either, although it was designed for the presenter to be seated beside it.

Disadvantages

- **Condition variable** – although OHPs are now to be found in many locations, many are older, well-used models which can be in a poor condition.
- **Crowded slide** – an acetate sheet from which OHP slides are produced can tempt the presenter to include too much material on one slide. A major advantage of the OHP is its potential for impact – overcrowding reduces this.
- **Headpost can obscure** – part of an OHP is the angled mirror mounted at the top of a column; this can obscure part of the screen image from some of the group unless particular care is taken in seating arrangements.
- **Keystoning** – the offputting effect of keystoning – the effect when the top of the projected image is wider horizontally than the base (usually the result of too acute an angle of projection) – can sometimes be difficult to rectify.
- **Older versions noisy** – older (and modern but cheaper) OHP models are cooled by a fan which can be very noisy.
- **Power required** – unlike for example, the flipchart, an electric power source is required. Most often this will not be a problem, but power failures do occur, or only unsuitable power sockets are available. Without power, or if the presenter does not have a converter plug, the OHP cannot be used.

ADVANTAGES	DISADVANTAGES
High visual impact	Condition variable
Large image	Crowded slide
OHP widely available	Headpost can obscure
Professional production	Keystoning
Slides easily portable	Older versions noisy
Usable in light	Power required
Used sitting or standing	

FLIPCHART, WHITEBOARD AND OVERHEAD PROJECTOR COMMON FACTORS

These three presentation aids have the following common factors, so their use is easily interchangeable.

- **Legibility** – there is little point in producing an aid if it is not legible to the audience. Legibility results from clarity, quality of writing, size of lettering, distance from the furthest member of the audience and so on. There can be no golden rule about the size of the lettering because of the variable factor of size of presentation location. A simple test is to write on a sheet of a flipchart using different sizes and then go and sit at the back of the room. The lettering you can read easily is the one you should use.
- **Writing on the medium** – writing or drawing on all the aids is different from making entries on, for example, an A4 sheet of paper. You must practise these different skills to ensure a professional approach that links with the legibility issue. There are also physical requirements concerned with writing – keeping lines horizontal, not talking to the flipchart, and even not writing on the projection screen (it does happen!).
- **Use of colour etc** – there are many opportunities when using visual aids to give impact to the message. This can be achieved by the use of colour, underlining, upper and lower case, boxing entries and so on.
- **Material media used** – all the aids being considered can be used in a variety of ways with a range of materials – writing, drawings, graphs, cards to hide or disclose – and such variety can add further impact.

FLIPCHART PREPARATION TIPS

Some methods can produce problems, but there are ways of avoiding them – here are some flipchart cribs and tips for you to use (many also apply to the whiteboard and the OHP).

Invisible outline (Faint pencil lines drawn across sheet)
Corner brief crib
Bookmarking
Tearing sheets from the pad
Finishing with an aid
Beware of pastel or pale yellow, light red and light green colours
Write more clearly and bigger than normally
Use graphics – drawings, images, pictures, cartoons
Use post-its as temporary postings
Avoid a cluttered chart
Consider lettering case
Talking and writing

Invisible outline

If you are unsure how much space will be used on a flipchart, are not used to writing freehand on flipcharts, are frightened that the writing will slide away from the horizontal, or are not sure about drawing a graphic in front of a group, prepare an outline before the session.

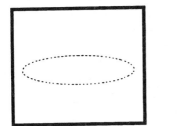 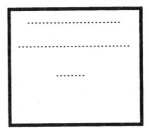

To help the writing along steady, horizontal lines, faint pencil lines can be drawn across the flipchart where required. Similarly, if key words are to be written on a flipchart during a session, these can be pencilled on before the session. If the pencil entries are made lightly, it is relatively easy for you to see them, but it is unlikely the audience, that is sitting some distance away, will see them at all.

Corner brief crib

If you have to move away from your brief to the flipchart during the session and are concerned that you may forget what to enter on the flipchart, in the top corner of the sheet lightly pencil the key words so that you, but not the audience, will be able to see them. This avoids having to carry your brief with you every time you move to the flipchart.

Bookmarking

There are times during a session when you are working with a flipchart sheet, whether pre-prepared or not, that you might wish to refer to a sheet which you have prepared and which is later in the pad. This sheet can be 'bookmarked' by placing a paper clip at the base of the sheet – this identifies the sheet and enables you to go to it immediately. If you have several sheets of this nature, two, three or more paper clips can be employed. Similarly, if you have just completed a sheet and you know you will have to refer back to it later in the session, 'bookmark' it for easy reference.

Tearing sheets from the pad

Only some pads of flipcharts have the tops of each sheet perforated for easy removal. Without a perforation, and following a certain 'law', tearing the sheet off the pad will almost certainly result in an imperfect tear – at worst only half the sheet tearing off! One pre-preparation can be to score the top of the sheet lightly with a metal ruler or craft knife and actually cut the first inch – this will ensure a smooth tear and no embarrassment.

Finishing with an aid

When you have finished with an aid, *get rid of it*. If you have used a flipchart sheet and you no longer need to refer to it, either detach it and fix it to the training room wall, flip it over the top of the chart, or tear it off and waste it. A whiteboard entry that is no longer required should be wiped off immediately after use (but be certain that you will not want to return to it). When an OHP slide has been used, switch the projector off – you can always switch it back on again if you require the slide again, or a new slide.

Failing to remove a past chart invites the participants to look at this rather than listen to your current input or observe your actions. The light from an OHP is very invasive and attracts attention, even more so if there is no slide on it.

Colours, sizes and graphics

Even if your favourite colours and shades tend towards the pastel or pale yellow, light red and light green, beware of these as they are not always clearly visible.

Write more clearly and bigger than you would normally do or think of doing. Small, rather unclear writing may be obvious to you at the flipchart, but 30 feet away at the rear of the group, it may mean nothing. To ensure clarity, write more slowly than you normally do – it may seem very slow to you, but the audience will probably not notice anything, especially if they can read what you have written.

Use graphics – drawings, images, pictures, cartoons – as much as possible, either supplementing the words on your chart or taking their place.

Post-its

When you are asking the group for ideas, suggestions, items of information, or anything similar that you would normally write on a flipchart which would then be posted on the wall, use post-its instead. Have the participants write their key words clearly on a post-it, then stick them all on a flipchart (or flipcharts) or whiteboard. A similar use can be made of pieces of acetate to be placed on the OHP – this would normally be a temporary activity.

Appearance and lettering case

There have been numerous anecdotal accounts and research data reported on the use of upper or lower case lettering – CAPITALS or non-capitals, different typefaces and so on. The appearance (both overall and detailed) of your flipchart can have a significant effect on whether the audience takes notice of or accepts the chart. A cluttered chart, crowded with detail, and produced with a monotonous, appearance will probably be dismissed by most of the audience as something they can't be bothered to read. On the other hand a clear, well-presented, attractive chart will have impact and will not only help the audience learn from the material but also remember it.

Talking and writing

One of the principal problems encountered by newcomers using a flipchart in front of an audience is when to talk and when to write. It has been suggested earlier that, in order to stop your lines flowing down to the right you stand facing the flipchart when writing. If you do this while you are talking:

1. You will be talking to the flipchart, not to the group, and your valuable message may be lost.
2. You have lost contact with the group for the time you are turned away from them.

So when you have to write on the flipchart stop talking, turn to the flipchart and write as quickly but as clearly as you can. The silence will seem interminable to you, but in fact will not be as long as it seems and the audience will not be disturbed unless you take a very long time. When you have finished writing, stand away from the flipchart to let the audience see what you have written. You will need to take these pauses into account when you are timing your presentation.

OTHER ASPECTS OF OHP USE

Keystoning

Keystoning is when the image projected from the OHP on to the screen is distorted, usually with the base being shorter than the top. This is caused by the angle of the projected light – if the projection is not horizontal, keystoning will occur. The opportunity to project horizontally is rarely possible as this would mean that the screen image was at the same height as the OHP – nobody would be able to see the image for the projector.

Fortunately most projection screens have a facility to tilt the top of the screen towards the projector, so making the relationship nearer the horizontal. An alternative, not always the most appropriate, is to tilt the OHP itself. Circumstances, however, do not always allow complete reduction of the effect, so you (and the audience) must be prepared to put up with some degree of keystoning. In fact, I have found audiences neither too aware nor too concerned about keystoning unless it is extreme.

Transparencies

Images are projected usually by means of a transparency or acetate square placed on the OHP. As mentioned earlier, these squares can be written on to produce slides, using either permanent or impermanent marker pens, dry lettering set or the computer. Although described as 'permanent' the writing produced by these pens can be removed with special solvents. Different transparency materials are available to make the slide: an acetate square is normally the medium on which pens are used; special film is available for printing out computer-produced slides, for both ink-jet and laser printers, to produce superior quality.

Computer programs are available to make the slide production reasonably simple. One advantage of this method is that series of slides can be made, thus keeping the slides together and avoiding one of the practical problems when you have a large number of slides.

Slides can also be made by specialist companies from a draft produced by the client – these companies often have more effective slide-making equipment than the individual or small company.

Visibility

One of the major problems encountered with using an OHP is the limit to visibility of the image on the screen. The OHP is usually placed on a small table and, because the OHP is a largish box with a head at the top of a column, both the box and the head can get in the way of the audience and the screen. The presenter can also get in the way. Considerable care must be taken in placing the OHP and screen to minimize poor visibility. Once you have positioned them, go and sit in different seats in the audience to see if you can see the projected image – have a colleague sit in your seat to make any necessary adjustments.

Sit or stand? Talking and writing

The principal advantage of the OHP over the flipchart and the whiteboard is that you can always face your audience, even when using your OHP. The image placed on the OHP is projected behind you and you have no reason to turn round to look at the screen – although many people still do this. If you want to see what is being projected, look at the OHP projection lens. This of course assumes that, at the start of the presentation you have ensured that the OHP is in focus and the slides are ready to be placed the correct way, ie face up with the bottom of the slide towards the screen and you). Adding to the projected image is simple – you write directly on the slide, not the screen, and again you continue to face the audience while you are doing this and the audience can see the writing developing.

The foregoing suggests that you will be seated beside the OHP, and this is the normal situation. But this does not stop you from standing and walking about when you feel you need to or have to, and you can do this while an image is being projected. Ensure in the latter case that you do not inhibit visibility of the screen.

Contents

The purpose of a visual aid is to support, not supplant, your verbal comments. So follow the principle of KISS – keep it short and simple – entering key words or phrases only for maximum impact and recall. Leave out all non-essential words and use abbreviations, after all you will be describing the full message while the abbreviated summary is on the aid.

SUMMARY OF OHP USE AND TECHNIQUES

Use relevant-sized lettering:
    up to 15 metres, lettering greater than 5mm in height
    15 to 20 metres, lettering greater than 10mm in height
    above 20 metres, lettering no less than 15mm in height
Mix both upper and lower case letters
Use clearest form of lettering available – freehand, dry lettering, laser printed
Never use typescript
Leave plenty of space between lines
Keep the slide uncluttered
Maximum of ten lines per slide – don't be a slave
Maximum of six or seven words per line – ditto
Frame for impact
Try white letters on a black background
Use colour freely – use dark colours
Always have a heading for your slide
Use graphics, symbols, speech marks and cartoons as often as possible –
    speech bubbles are particularly useful and impactive
Check OHP is correctly focused and the bulb works – check spare
Avoid keystoning
Use the various transparency preparation methods
Ensure visibility from all parts
Decide whether to sit or stand
Talking and writing
Contents – KISS

VIDEO OHPs

This is the electronic version of the episcope which is used for the projection of images of solid objects, but one which has a wider versatility, particularly with objects of greater depth. An episcope functions well with two-dimensional objects, but when any height is introduced the depth of focus leaves a lot to be desired. The video OHP can cope better in this respect and can also operate in brighter light conditions. However, because the image is projected on to a TV monitor, unless you have a very large monitor or a data projector, the facility is limited to smaller groups.

The video OHP differs from the traditional one in a number of ways. A video camera mounted at the top of a column is used to view the object – two or three dimensional, static or moving. Obviously there is a limit to the size of the object that can be projected, but the instrument is certainly useful for small objects or parts, or perhaps models of larger objects.

AUDIO EQUIPMENT

In presentations this term is generally used to mean audio cassette players and associated equipment. The audio cassette has a useful, albeit limited use in presentations. The video attracts much more interest with its combination of sound and movement, and its familiarity to the viewers as part of everyday life.

But the audio cassette used appropriately can be a further support to the presenter. The playing of a short excerpt from a cassette produced either by the presenter or, more usually, some expert in the subject, can change the atmosphere and pace of the session, affording the audience a break from the presenter – and vice versa! Sometimes part of the presentation is complex and the use of exact wording is essential – the pre-recorded audio cassette can be used for this purpose very effectively and accurately.

It is also a useful medium for playing music, perhaps background music while the participants are assembling – a time when both the presenter and the audience may be feeling a little strange and strained. Suitable music can help to relieve this atmosphere.

Another use for the audio cassette, borrowed from training and self-development activities, is to play it on a car cassette player. Recorded presentations over a range of subjects, either by the individual who would be giving the presentation or by a professional speaker on a commercially produced cassette, can be played back while the listener is travelling in the car. Played on a personal cassette player it can be listened to in the comfort of your home or while travelling by bus, train or plane.

Audio cassettes certainly do not fully take the place of the personal presentation or the video programme, but offer a relatively cheap, convenient method when others are not available.

Combined audiovisual aids

Cassettes can be combined in one projector with 35mm slides as a table-top projector for small groups. The projector projects either manually or automatically a programme of 35mm slides to the accompaniment of a verbal presentation on cassette which can be electronically synchronized with the slides. The size of the group can be increased as many of these combination player-projectors can also be simply converted to project the image on a screen.

Be very careful that the slides are all properly mounted and inserted in the projector carriage, otherwise a jam can occur, sometimes with the commentary continuing. Once the process has started you have only little control, other than stopping and restarting the programme. Returning to a subject as the result of, say, a question from a member of the group can be extremely difficult and the programme, once established, is confined to that material. However, this approach can be useful where an individual or small group come together without the need for (or availability of) the original presenter, and custom-made, self-produced programmes are quite simple to produce if you have the required electronic pulse equipment.

THE COMPUTER

As in many fields, the computer is starting to make its mark as a valuable item of presentation equipment. Its use in presentations is often limited by the size of the monitor, but again the data projector can help here.

Its most impactive use is in remote presentations, where an individual or a small group work through a computer program in their own time and at their own pace, going back to sections that were not understood or remembered. The computer comes into its own in logical presentations where the message is relatively fixed and procedural – you cannot argue with a computer, so the program assemblers must ensure that the program is correct in every way. When several monitors are networked in a company a number of viewers in different locations can watch the program at the same time. Messages or questions can also be introduced from the control computer.

An obvious use for a computer-based presentation is to employees who are to operate a computer system. Before the introduction of the system (and perhaps detailed instruction), the operators can view a presentation that uses parts of the new system itself as a demonstration.

The use of the computer to produce OHP slides was mentioned in the previous chapter. There are special software programs for this purpose, offering a very wide range of format, lettering and frames, the computer-generated slide being printed out on special film sheets. The result is a, clear, crisp slide which, if linked with a colour printer, can be produced with most of the recommended features. The slide can be retained on the computer so that it is a simple process to revise information as necessary, or to duplicate the slide for multi-sets. You can batch the slides in similar subject groups or even have a complete presentation set of slides together in one file. Gone are the days of losing a slide and having to spend hours constructing a new one – the computer offers this facility in a matter of minutes.

Most of the presentation programs, in addition to offering text facilities, include a clipart and/or picture library so that words and pictures can be easily mixed on a slide. Material from other programs can also be copied or moved, again saving time in not having to repeat existing material.

With technological advances there is less need to produce 'hard-copy' acetates from the computer-produced slides. The slides are produced directly as a computer document by means of a special application such as Microsoft PowerPoint®. This program offers a vast variety of facilities for slide production – a large range of fonts; an extended series of slide templates in colour and black and white; adding clipart and photographs; adding bullets and all the usual word processing facilities. Figure 5.1 shows in monochrome a multicoloured slide I produced (using the methods described above) for a slide presentation on evaluation. Producing a hard-copy acetate in this range of colours would demand a very advanced printer, but by using the computer directly as the slide projector, the colours can be retained.

Clipart, pictures and photographs can be added to the slides directly within the PowerPoint program or imported and edited from clipart, etc collections produced by Serif, IMSI, Management Graphics and others on CD-ROMs. Some of these CDs contain several thousand graphics over a wide range of subjects.

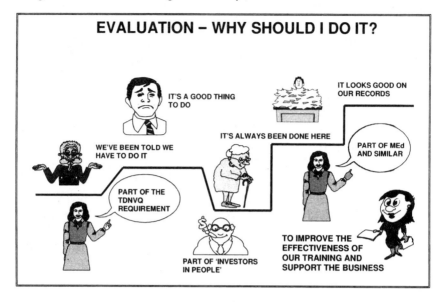

Figure 5.1   *Example of a simplified PowerPoint® slide*

A series of slides can be amalgamated into a slide show, the slides being progressed by a simple movement of the computer mouse and projected on the computer monitor or, via supplementary equipment, onto a large screen. One of the disturbing aspects of the normal OHP slide show is the break between slides, either with a bright clear image being left on the projector, or the OHP being turned off between each slide. This is circumvented with a computer program by:

■ adding a black slide at the end of the presentation to focus the audience's attention back to the speaker;
■ applying a slide transition so that one slide fades or dissolves into the next;
■ controlling the speed of slide transitions from slow to fast, or in increments of seconds.

Particular effects are also possible by means of a program such as PowerPoint. These include:

varying the colour of bullets;
varying the colour of each entry on the slides;
dimming the colour of successive bullets.

Possibly the most effective of the program techniques, and one that equates with the physical (and often unsuccessful) OHP slide additive technique, is the process of slide build. This allows you to reveal bulleted lines on a slide one at a time, not only by revealing an existing entry, but also by having also the line drop-down into the list. The drop-down facility has a range of options, from allowing the new line to simply appear, through flying down from the top of the slide, from the left or right or bottom; fading; appearing as above but in a 'checkerboard' display; etc.

The final principal effect is to hide a slide. This allows you the choice of using or omitting a particular slide in the sequence, just as you would physically set aside an acetate slide that you decided to omit.

The problems of using somebody else's computer if you have to move away from your home location have even been solved. Included with the software is a special part that allows a copy of the slide show to be made, accompanied by a facility to use the program disc on another computer, whether or not that computer has the PowerPoint program installed. A 3.5 inch disk weighing only several milligrams has considerable advantages over a heavy OHP – however portable – and a batch of acetate squares!

LARGE-SCREEN PROJECTION

The principal problem until recently in using a computer for a presentation has been the small size of the computer monitor screen. This has now been remedied by the increasing availability of large-scale projectors that can be linked to the computer. These can be either CRT or LCD, and they project the computer image on to a large screen in full, original colour. Earlier models required considerable expertise in setting-up and balancing the colours and images, but much of this is now automatic. The projectors can be single or multilens and their availability is increasing rapidly, particularly in conference centres and hotels specializing in providing conference or presentation facilities. They have many advantages, including:

- an image so large that it can be seen from anywhere, in even a large room;
- the speaker has few worries about interfering with the line of vision;
- full colour provision;
- use for fully automated or speaker-controlled slide shows;
- demonstration of all the computer techniques described above;
- can project slide shows from computer-filed sets of slides on desktop or laptop computers;
- demonstrate a greater professionalism than OHPs.

The use of a computer with a large-screen projector is simplicity itself, the speaker standing unobtrusively at the side of the screen, controlling the presentation by simple clicks of the computer mouse. A lectern becomes less obtrusive in such circumstances and this can be used to hold the speaker's notes and the operating mouse. I have found this method of slide presentation much more effective and easier than the physical use of an OHP and a set of slides, once you become accustomed to the medium and its use is strongly recommended.

SLIDE PROJECTOR

The slide projector is used for photographic slides or transparencies, usually from 35mm film. The slides are generally photographs of objects or places, but they can be of drawings and charts. Projection normally has to be in a darkened room on to a screen, although special screens through which the image can be back-projected do not need as dark a room. Some years ago slides were fed into the projector by hand and the slide-carrier moved manually, but now large slide cassettes can be attached to the projector for remote control or automatic operation.

The location of the slides in a cassette means that there is a fixed sequence of projection although, with the remote control, reversing is possible. This sequencing is no problem for slides used in a fixed, formal presentation, but it does restrict the flexibility of the equipment.

This is one of the more costly techniques as requirements – if a professional result is to be obtained – are a versatile camera and ancillary equipment, effective processing of the slide film, satisfactory slide editing and mounting, a quality projector and screen. However, when all these factors have been taken into account, the result can be a highly professional presentation aid with considerable variation, using words, drawings, pictures and other graphics.

VIDEO PLAYER

This equipment has grown in value for presentations with the increased availability of good quality videos, and these can support a live presentation in a very effective manner. The process is simple and very familiar to many people as a video image projected on the normal type of television receiver or monitor, although large-screen monitors are available and the data projectors mentioned earlier can project images on to very large screens. Use on the familiar size of monitor is the most common, however, and this restricts use to small groups.

The video can be used in conjunction with presentations:

- as a stand-alone event in which the video replaces the live presenter completely, apart from an introduction;
- at the start of the event to introduce the subject;
- during the presentation at various stages to reinforce the presenter's input, to change the pace and impact of the session or to take the place of part of the presenter's input;
- at the end of the event to act as a recall instrument or to summarize the presentation content;
- after the event, by the event participants back at work to recall the messages.

One problem concerned with the use of this technique may be the availability of a suitable video, although the range of subjects available on video is now very extensive. An alternative, particularly if a number of similar presentations is to be made or the video can be sent round the organization as a stand-alone, is to make your own video. This can be with or without the support of a professional video producer working to the required brief or, if speed is more important than quality, a 'home' video can be produced with a good domestic camcorder. With thorough planning and a little skill, an acceptable video can be produced this way, and will be exactly to your requirements. The amateurism of the 'actors' can sometimes detract slightly but, more often than not, known participants make the video lifelike.

Videos are much more flexible than the usually accepted format of television programmes and during a presentation can be:

- played straight through, preferably followed by some form of discussion;
- played as required for the purposes of support;
- interrupted at relevant intervals to involve the group;
- used in a scenario form to trigger discussion.

'Trigger' videos lend themselves well to home production, being short scenarios of two or three minutes in which something is started but not completed. The trigger is then stopped and the group asked questions relating to the video to get their views and agreement of 'what should happen next?'.

Used inventively the video can be raised from a simple film replacement, or be included in a programme to give the presenter a rest or fill in some time!

HANDOUTS

Handouts are not normally thought of when a list of presentation aids is being considered, but they are probably the most common aid in use. There are three opportunities – or a combination of the three – for using handouts relating to an event.

■ They can be issued *before* the event, to prepare the members for the more detailed or deeper live session. If participants read the handout and perhaps perform any exercises included before the event, in theory they are starting the event at the same, or at a common minimum level. One problem, however, can be that the audience, having read the handout, takes the attitude or believes that they know all about the subject, and as the presentation proceeds can be thinking, or even saying, 'We already know that!' Or as the session is proceeding, they can be reading the handout, sometimes with the intention of checking that the presenter is saying what is in the handout. This is a caveat for handout producers – ensure that the written content does not conflict with the spoken content (this is not unknown!). But a pre-event handout can be valuable as a time controller, ensuring that the limited time for the presentation is used effectively.

■ Handouts can be used *during* an event to reinforce the presenter's presentation, but are most effectively used *after* that part of the presentation to which reference is required. The handout can be issued and the audience given a short time to read it: this can raise questions from the audience or a discussion on the topic, if this is what is desired and time is available.

■ The most common use is to issue the handout *at the end* of the event, with the hope that the participants will read and re-read them and perhaps use them in their implementation of the subject. However, post-event use varies considerably, and I have encountered comments from:
  - 'I threw them away before I even left the room';
  - 'When I got back to work I put them in a drawer and have never looked at them again';

through

  - 'I look at them occasionally to remind me of the content of the presentation';

to

- 'I frequently refer to them to remind me of the material and also when I am constructing a presentation of my own on the subject';
- 'I use them as handouts on my own presentations'.

There are usually reasons why the first two comments are made (perhaps all too frequently), ranging from badly written handouts to irrelevant or incorrect material. But the most likely reason is that the handouts are written in a format that does not encourage reference. If a handout (other than certain types of technical handout) is written on more than two sheets of A4 paper, the likelihood of it being read decreases rapidly with the increasing number of pages. Perhaps the ideal is one side of one sheet of A4. To achieve this the handout content must be considered carefully and the producer must restrain any desire to produce literary perfection.

The guidelines include:

- using one side of one sheet of A4 paper wherever possible;
- including plenty of 'white space' for easy reading and impact of what is written;
- using bullet lists rather than textual paragraphs;
- in the bullet lists, using key words and phrases rather than grammatically complete sentences;
- using language as simple as possible, taking the subject into account;
- using lower case rather than upper case – research has shown that this is easier to read.

Obviously there will be instances when more substantial handouts have to be produced, but bear in mind the general rule that the longer a handout, the less likely it will be read. Many of the best handouts I have seen have in fact been copies of OHP slides used during the session.

Finally, remember that presentation aids are only *aids*. They should not be used instead of briefs or scripts, should not take the place of a presentation if it has been agreed that a presentation is the most appropriate way of presenting the subject, and should be used as supplementary aids, not crutches.

SOME ACTIVITIES TO CONSIDER

ACTIVITY: Consider any recent presentations you have given and review either:

■   whether the presentation would have been improved by the use of aids and what types; or
■   whether the aids used were the most effective and appropriate or whether other aids would have been more appropriate.

Discuss these considerations with the rest of the group and come to some group conclusions about the use of training aids.

ACTIVITY: If you are soon to make a presentation, consider the range of presentation aids available and which ones you would like to use and would be able to use.

Discuss your views with the remainder of the group and be prepared to report your group findings to the full group.

ACTIVITY: As an alternative to introducing presentation aids in an input session, divide the group into smaller groups and ask each group to consider a particular aid, identify as many factors as possible about it, and be prepared to present these considerations to the other groups. A 'sweep-up' summary can then be given to cover any important aspects omitted.

6
—

Constructing and Using Visual Aids

This chapter:

- describes how to produce yourself a range of visual aids and how to use them effectively
- gives guidance on methods of presenting charts, diagrams and graphs in an effective manner.

THE CONSTRUCTION AND USE OF VISUAL AIDS

In addition to being able to use the equipment effectively, you must also learn to produce complete visual aids yourself and use them effectively. Some mention has been made about some of the common aspects of the three aids under discussion – legibility, impact, the use of colour and so on. However, there are some special techniques that can be used to improve the effectiveness and the impact of the aids. Some of these are applicable to the flipchart, some to the whiteboard, some to the OHP and some to all.

These latter include:

- disclosure techniques and
- additive techniques.

DISCLOSURE TECHNIQUES

One of the problems of showing a complete visual aid, whether flipchart, whiteboard or OHP slide, is that while you are talking about the entries many of the audience are ahead of you – they can read faster than you can talk and extend the entries. This means that they may not be listening effectively to what you are saying.

Flipchart disclosure

One technique for avoiding this is to disclose only part of the chart, the part to which you are referring. The chart or slide is prepared before the session and, apart from the chart heading, all the entries are covered up.

With the flipchart, the most effective method of covering in this way is to have rectangles of card fixed over the entries. Fixing these is easy with a dry adhesive such as BluTack.

The principal problem with this method is that you are unable to see the entries under the covering cards – unless you are so *au fait* with the charts that you can remember all the entries. It is safer to have a prompt on each card – a pencil entry on the card describing the hidden material will be seen by you but not the audience.

Whiteboard disclosure

If a dry adhesive is used frequently on a whiteboard to disclose entries, the surface of the board will deteriorate. Many whiteboards are magnetic, and here the cards can be held by small magnets. It must be said that the disclosure method of pre-prepared material is not as successful with the whiteboard as with the other media – the pens used to write on the board are intended to be erased, but this erasure can be accidentally done by the disclosure cards.

OHP disclosure

Several variations are available for the OHP. The cards can be simply laid over the slide entries without any fixing agent, although there is always the risk of slippage and premature disclosure. A sheet of opaque A4 paper can cover the items, being pulled down as required. This latter method has several caveats. If the paper is placed over the slide, the entries beneath it cannot be seen and the sliding movement makes pencil entries unworkable. Also, as the sheet nears the bottom of the slide, because of the paper overhang and movement caused by the OHP fan, the paper can fall off the slide. These can be easily avoided by placing the paper sheet *under* the OHP acetate slide. The slide holds the paper sheet down and the entries on the slide can be seen. This method of disclosure, however, makes the disclosure inflexible as entries *must* be uncovered in their top-down order.

The card method of disclosure can be made more effective on the OHP slide if the card is anchored. One end of each card can be anchored with adhesive tape acting as a hinge, the card being swung to the side when required.

Obviously the card covers need not be rectangles: if the chart or slide contains graphics rather than words, the cover can be roughly the shape of the graphic – the rough shape can make the covered graphic even more interesting!

ADDITIVE TECHNIQUES

The additive technique, as its name suggests, is the opposite to the disclosure method and starts with a blank flipchart, whiteboard area or OHP slide. Obviously little preparation can be made before the session and, in fact, the method is intended to be used as an immediate technique.

Flipchart and whiteboard additions

With the flipchart and the whiteboard, the straightforward addition during a session starts with a blank area. Material is added as the result of asking the audience questions or simply writing on the area. The card technique for disclosure can be used in reverse – pre-prepared cards can be added to the area as required by fixing them with a dry adhesive or magnet. For example, a group might be asked to suggest the ten advantages of using such-and-such. As the advantages are called out, you can place the relevant card on the area, not necessarily in a neat, logical table. Or, as you start to describe the ten advantages of using such-and-such, someone can place the card on the area as the advantage is introduced. The principal objection to the method of adding cards from the suggestions by the participants is that you obviously have the information cards already, and can be accused of wasting time by waiting for the information to be called out. Another problem for the presenter is when the audience does not call out all the required information – the missing information cards have then to be produced and the presenter can again be accused of manipulation.

OHP additions

Similar methods can be used with the OHP slide, with written additions being made to a clear acetate sheet or prepared acetate pieces placed on the OHP. A more permanent additive slide can be produced by using the hinged disclosure cards. In this instance the cards are folded away from the slide and folded on to it when the item is required.

An alternative additive method for the OHP can be to have a series of slides which are progressively placed on the OHP to build up a composite picture. Registration must be accurate – marks can be made on each slide – or the slides can be bound together at one edge so that they can be hinged over as required. The former method permits flexibility but has the non-registration danger, whereas the latter is inflexible but ensures accurate registration.

Few visual aids are themselves explicit enough to stand alone without description, and as we have seen this is not their purpose. But if we reach the stage when the presenter has to stop to explain the visual aid intended to support the presentation, then something has gone wrong with the aid.

This usually occurs when charts, graphs and diagrams are shown and the presenter wants to make them as comprehensive as possible. The end result is often a chart crammed with too much information for the viewer to take in. The advice must be, as with the spoken and written word, KISS – Keep it short and simple.

GRAPHS, CHARTS AND DIAGRAMS

Tabulated data

Many of the projected aids at a meeting presentation are concerned with the visual presentation of data, usually obtained from tables contained in reports. The naive may think that the most effective way of showing this data is to reproduce the table – in this way, all the data is there and all the presenter has to do is to:

(a) display the data for the members to read;
(b) explain the data – what it is, where it came from etc;
(c) explain the analyses of the data.

The following table of data lists the number of Unit Trusts arranged during an 11-year period.

UNIT TRUST PURCHASES			
Millions of currency units			
	ORDINARY	SPECIAL	COMPLEX	TOTAL
1970	104,883	29,169	12,888	146,940
1971	110,322	34,088	14,000	158,410
1972	113,992	31,066	14,092	159,150
1973	128,534	36,304	14,308	179,146
1974	148,024	47,468	14,624	210,116
1975	186,970	47,170	14,592	248,732
1976	187,386	52,438	14,156	253,980
1977	189,388	61,636	14,102	265,126
1978	207,888	72,954	13,348	294,190
1979	227,000	78,658	12,908	318,566
1980	245,960	94,006	13,210	353,176
Totals	**1,850,347**	**584,957**	**152,228**	**2,587,532**

If you wished to use this data produced on an OHP or 35 mm slide in the form of the table itself, very little benefit would result. The problems are:

■ there is too much detail to be included in one projected slide;
■ breaking the table into several slides would make description and comparison too difficult;
■ the image is one of many large figures which dissolve into each other and produce a glazing of the eyes;
■ if the audience is not fully conversant with the data, they cannot be expected to analyse the figures from this mass of information suddenly presented to them.

You are then faced with two problems to solve.

1. Which aspects of analysis do I want or need to demonstrate?
2. Which method of presentation is going to be the most effective for this kind of data, ie what form of visual aid?

Among other factors, the table demonstrates change. The horizontal totals show the change of the monetary value of purchases of unit trusts over a period of eleven years; the vertical totals show the relative size of purchases between ordinary, special and complex unit trusts. Both these aspects can be compared in a visual aid.

In addition, the relative sizes of purchases of the three types of trust can be compared in each year; each figure can be converted to a percentage of its own column, its own year or full totals of the decade or the type of trust.

Any or all of these can be converted from the table to a visual aid, and a further choice of the style of visual aid becomes available.

Chart forms

Any information can be presented in the form of a 'chart', a description commonly used for a range of charts, diagrams, drawings etc, each one being most effective when used for a particular purpose. The charts in most common use, and described here, include pie, bar, column and line charts and graphs.

Pie charts

A pie chart is a circle divided into segments, each segment showing a particular area of the total. This area is shown as a relative-sized part of the whole. Because all the information is included in the one circle, the pie chart is ideally suited to show at a glance a comparison of the components.

However, with our table in mind, the value of the pie would be destroyed if too many components were included; the pie is at its best with a simple approach and an optimum of six components.

Positioning the components can be important. The eye is used to moving in a clockwise direction and to do so starts at about the 12 or 1 o'clock positions. It may therefore be appropriate to place the segment which contains the most important information in this position, although this is not essential if the segments are clearly indicated.

The segments will be graded in size according to the size of the component being compared. This should be produced accurately, and if approximate sizes are used these should still demonstrate the relative differences in size.

Colours or shadings should be used to differentiate between each segment, although this is not completely essential as each segment is divided by a line. However, shading of some nature ensures that the segmentation is obvious, an essential element in a visual aid. Figure 6.1 shows a standard pie chart.

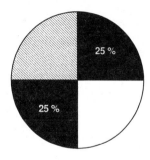

Figure 6.1 *A standard pie chart*

A number of variations on the standard pie chart are possible, the most useful and most frequently used being the exploded pie chart. In this version, the segment representing the component that the presenter wishes to make prominent is separated from the remainder of the pie.

The separated segment can be at any place in the pie and becomes more prominent if it is positively shaded. Figure 6.2 is a representation of an exploded pie chart.

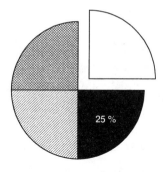

Figure 6.2 *An exploded pie chart*

Bar charts

Pie charts have the advantages of being relatively simple to construct, they need not be accurate in their drawing and can present simple information in an impactive manner. This makes them very suitable for projected slide images. Another advantage is that rarely do they have to be drawn by hand – every computer, however simple – has a software graphics program which enables pie charts to be constructed easily. (Ease of construction applies to virtually all methods of presenting charts, so you have no argument for not using these aids by suggesting that there was insufficient time to produce them.)

But pie charts, because of their simplicity, cannot show the finer details. Of course, captions can be placed alongside or within a segment giving information, but this starts to complicate the representation and make it unclear.

A chart which is useful in describing changes and comparisons in rather more detail is the bar chart. In its standard form it consists of a graph, but instead of depicting points on the graph as in a line graph, each component is described with a block or bar.

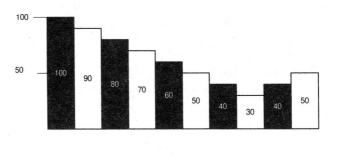

Figure 6.3 *A simple bar chart*

The bar chart in Figure 6.3 is presented with the bars vertical. This is the most frequently used method of drawing a bar chart, but many people consider it is more effective when drawn so that the bars project horizontally from the left-hand vertical as shown in Figure 6.4.

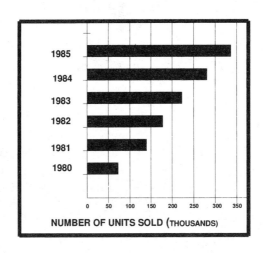

Figure 6.4 *A simple bar chart (horizontal)*

The space below each bar in the vertical approach is strictly limited, particularly if there are an appreciable number of bars. In the horizontal version much more text can be added, written if necessary within the bars or, if space has been left between each bar, in that space. With simple information, such as the year in Figure 6.3, additional space is not necessary so the vertical bar is satisfactory.

Graphs

The immediate reaction of most people when a chart is suggested as a means of describing numerical data is to think of a graph of some kind. Line charts or graphs consist of information plotted on the vertical and horizontal axes, with a point placed at the intersection of these axes. The points are then joined by a continuous straight or curved line.

Some simple rules can be followed to ensure that the chart is as clear as possible. Usually the vertical scale represents magnitude or level and the horizontal scale time. The stages should be consistent in size and continuity – if some data is missing, a space should be left rather than its absence ignored; otherwise the trends will be distorted.

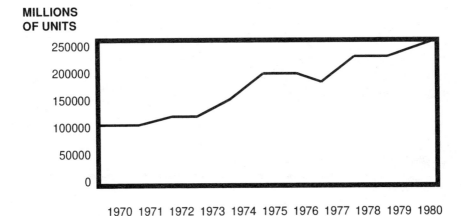

Figure 6.5a *A line graph*

Figure 6.5a is a typical line graph with the points joined by straight lines – the easiest although not always the best way of joining the points. In this case, the yearly totals of all units purchased are plotted against their monetary values. Figure 6.5b demonstrates the more solid type of single-line graph in which the space below the line is filled to give greater impact.

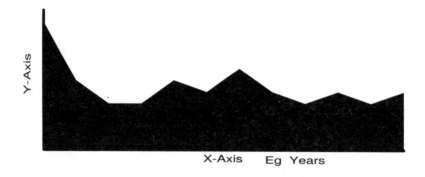

Figure 6.5b *A block line graph*

There is no need to start the vertical scale always at zero; this can throw all the information into the top part of the graph, thus losing impact. Instead start with a scale point one step lower than the first point, or with the first point at the intersection of the vertical and horizontal axes.

Graph constructors must always be aware of possible distortions introduced by using scales which are inconsistent with the information range, variable scale steps, omitted steps and exaggerated scales – all of these manipulate the appearance of the graph and contaminate the visual impression. Figure 6.5c demonstrates this, the positions taken from Figure 6.5a. (These distortions are frequently used in an attempt to give false impressions, and can often be successful – political presentations are frequent perpetrators of this deception.)

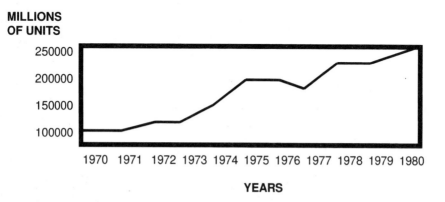

Figure 6.5c *An adjusted line graph*

Sometimes the presenter wants to produce a line graph showing the changing factors of a number of components, for example the growth of each of the unit trust types – ordinary, special and complex. Frequently this causes problems in the vertical size of the graph when, as in the case of the units, there is a large variation in the levels – the low-level complex figures will be close to the base of the graph and there will be a large gap between those and the figures for the ordinary units which will be at the top of the graph. On occasions this can be avoided by having two vertical scales for two components, one at the left, the other at the right. This works with two components, but with more than this there are unacceptable complications for a visual aid constructor.

Unless a line graph is demanded, in these multiple cases it may be more appropriate to use another chart medium, for example a bar or column chart. However, in spite of the non-aesthetic nature of the multiple line graph with wide differences, these very differences may show the significance of the comparison between the components. Figure 6.6 demonstrates this.

The principal variation in the line graph is the replacement of the straight lines joining the points by a line curving to follow the direction of the next point. This produces a pleasant image and a more accurate demonstration of the movement, but requires good draughtsmanship to ensure these aspects.

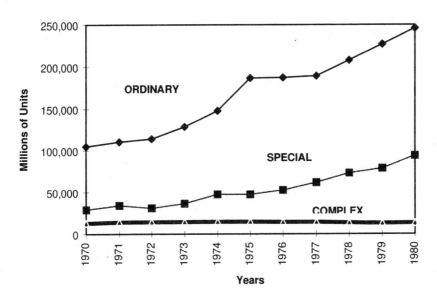

Figure 6.6 *A multi-component graph*

There are of course numerous other types of charts, many for specialist use, and if the pie, bar or line charts do not satisfy your particular needs, you will need to refer to one of the specialist books on the subject. But remember that the more complex the chart the more difficult it is for the audience to understand, and the more explanation you will have to give. Again bear in mind KISS!

SOME ACTIVITIES TO CONSIDER

ACTIVITY

1. **Disclosure on the flipchart.** Using a prepared flipchart with a number of items covered by pieces of card, held by BluTack, disclose the items.
2. **Disclosure on the whiteboard.** Disclose items written on a whiteboard covered by card fixed with magnetic strips by removing the cards.
3. **Disclosure on the OHP.** Using a slide with several items included, demonstrate disclosure by sliding a piece of paper, first on top of the slide, then underneath.
4. **Disclosure on the OHP.** Have a prepared slide with hinged cards, disclosing items one by one.
5. **Additive techniques with the flipchart and the whiteboard.** Demonstrate adding to a blank flipchart or whiteboard by using effective written techniques.
6. **Additive techniques with the OHP – pieces of acetate.** Using small pieces of acetate, produce a composite slide by placing the pieces on the OHP platen.
7. **Additive techniques with the OHP – composite slide.** Demonstrate the formation of a final, composite slide by placing several acetate sheets on top of each other.
8. **Additive techniques with the OHP – hinged additions.** As with the hinged cards disclosure technique, add to a blank slide by folding *in* the hinged cards.

ACTIVITY Identify some tabulated data that you have used in a previous presentation or want to include in a future one and convert the data into various types of charts to decide which would be the most relevant for that particular type of data.

ACTIVITY Divide the group into smaller groups and give each group a different set of data, information or figure set. Ask each group to devise the most appropriate presentation aid for the material they have been given, for presentation to and discussion with the other groups.

7

—

Personal Presentation
Jacqueline Twyman

This chapter:

- offers hints, tips and guidance on the effective presentation of your most important visual aid – yourself.

FIRST IMPRESSIONS LAST

First impressions are lasting impressions and are the basis on which all other impressions are formed. When making a presentation it is important to realize that you are your best visual aid. From the moment your audience first sees you, your competence is being judged by the way you look. When they are waiting for you to speak the chances are that your audience will have been observing you and be well on their way to making up their minds about you.

A positive first impression therefore:

- stands you in very good stead
- arouses interest
- is likely to make the audience more anxious to hear what you have to say.

If what they see is creating a negative impression, however, you are unlikely to have their full attention.

GETTING READY

Two of the most effective ways of ensuring that your audience's reaction to you is positive before you have even begun to speak include presenting yourself effectively and creating an impact.

Presenting yourself effectively

Preparation for effective self-presentation ranks equally with preparation of your content, handouts and any equipment you may be using. You must be aware of what appearance you are going to have on stage as well as what you are going to say, the physical evidence that you will leave behind with your audience and familiarity with all your other visual aids.

You might not believe, or even disagree, that self-presentation ranks highly when you give a presentation. After all, you have been invited (or press-ganged) into giving a presentation and so you will be on stage on merit (or because it's your 'turn').

So why is it important? Research has shown that the first impressions we make within 30 seconds of meeting someone are based:

- 55 per cent on appearance
- 38 per cent on behaviour (body language, manner of speaking)
- 7 per cent on content.

Figure 7.1 demonstrates this graphically.

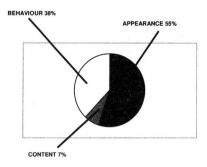

Figure 7.1 *First impressions*

Creating an impact

Which of the two representations just given made a greater impact on you – the bullet list or the figure? In all probability it was the figure. But whichever it was, the clear signal given from these percentages is that the non-verbal, visual message has a greater initial impact than the oral one – seeing is believing.

The image that you project as a presenter has a threefold purpose.

1. It conveys the impression you wish to make
2. It is a form of non-verbal communication from which people make value judgements
3. It can be used as a tool with which to gain your objectives

The right impression. It does not follow that because you have been invited to make a presentation that you are the world's expert on that subject. But you do not want your audience to see you as nervous and unsure. Rather, you will want to come across as capable and in control.

Value judgements. We all have expectations of what others should look like – from accountants to zoologists – and you need to make sure you project an image of what you really are, not just a stereotype. You might be highly qualified or only just starting out as a speaker – whichever it is, and whatever the tangible elements of your success to date, these do not accompany you on stage.

What are the symbols of your success – education, house, car, holidays? When you stand up or sit in front of an audience, only your appearance is visible and this is the most direct and immediate form of your communication with them. If you get this impact from your appearance wrong, you may lose your credibility and, therefore, your audience. Therefore it is essential to concentrate on getting it *right*.

Image as a tool. You are the message medium and the content of your message is best conveyed through a professional, positive appearance; clear and correct speech; and a thorough knowledge of your subject. You are (or should be) the 'fount of all knowledge' for the time you are presenting and you need your image to get your message across.

MANAGING THE IMPACT

The initial impact that you create with your image can be managed successfully throughout your presentation. When you look positive and feel positive about yourself, this will be transmitted to your audience, who will react to you more positively than otherwise. In order to build on your initial impact you need to put into practice the principles behind what makes a good first impression. You do this through:

> - your appearance
> - your behaviour
> - your content

Your appearance

Creating a positive impact is dependent on looking the part, which in turn means you *are* the part as far as the audience is concerned. This is the non-verbal message that should be received by the audience who are consequently more like to listen closely, trust what you are saying, and certainly assume that you know what you are talking about.

A positive image and a positive impact increase your self-confidence while making your presentation.

Looking the part (and then being able to forget about how you look):

> - gets the right attention
> - states who you are
> - promotes your cause
> - reflects your self-esteem, personality and attitude to the occasion
> - increases your confidence
> - does not distract

Getting the right attention. The introductions have been made and you are ready to begin your presentation. Your image is all your audience has to go on so far. It should be striking without being excessive.

Stating who you are. There is an important credibility factor here. Whether the audience expects a heavy exposition on accounting or a light-hearted activity session, honour their feelings by dressing *up* for them. They will be more flattered than if you try to be 'one of them' and this will signal your success.

Make sure, however, that you do not alienate the audience by appearing unapproachable and presenting an image that is unattainable by them or not in keeping with their expectations. You should aim to gain acceptance from an audience by association with them (see dress codes later).

Promoting your cause. If you have been asked, say, to introduce the work of your department as part of a team-building exercise, use the opportunity to let your image proclaim efficiency, your commitment to and control of the situation.

Reflecting yourself. The saying 'She did herself proud' is especially apt here. The reverse, 'She let herself down', is certainly not how you want to be remembered.

Increasing your confidence. When you do not have to worry about how you look, you can more easily concentrate on the other factors that will make your presentation successful.

Concentration, not distraction. A striking, but not excessive image on stage does not distract the audience, rather it aids their concentration. You are using your image to control your role as presenter, fulfilling your audience's expectations and successfully imparting your information.

A positive self-image resulting from looking the part (which could also be termed 'your best look') means that your own perceived image is, correctly, your audience's received image. At this stage you might ask yourself what image you have of yourself and whether you think it matches the audience's expectations. Figure 7.2 summarizes a successful image.

Figure 7.2 *The circle of success*

Other points to consider

Is your appearance appropriate?

A headteacher proposing increased staffing levels to the board of governors; a sales manager introducing a major new product to the sales team; an instructor training in the art of outdoor survival – these presenters would obviously project totally different images to maintain credibility with their audience.

As an image consultant I often ask my audiences what their reaction would be if I stood before them in wellington boots, jeans, anorak and a bobble hat. Their reply is usually that the outfit is perfect workwear for, say, a gardener and what they might expect their local horticultural expert to wear, but it wouldn't be very convincing for an indoor presentation.

You might also need to think about the time of day of your presentation. Slightly more formal wear would be appropriate for evenings, with perhaps more emphasis on jewellery and make-up for women. This does not, however, give you *carte blanche* to deck yourself out in your latest clubbing gear or your one, extravagant, designer tie.

Is there a dress code?

In addition to being appropriate to your audience, your appearance should be appropriate to the culture of the organization that invited you. Dress codes apply equally to presentations as they do to black-tie dinners. But in this instance I mean any dress code, not necessarily a formal one, and certainly not in the context of a 'uniform'. However, if you are presenting in a city institution you may well be expected to conform by appearing in a sombre suit which would look highly out of place in the more relaxed atmosphere of an advertising agency, for instance. Another example is whether a woman wearing trousers is acceptable or frowned upon.

There has been a movement recently towards an American import to Britain – 'dressing down days'. These are usually Fridays, when corporate staff are encouraged to wear more casual clothes than usual to work. Along with your other pre-presentation checks, it would be worth your while to enquire whether such days exists where you are making your presentation, although this does not necessarily mean that *you* have to 'dress down'.

Are you in uniform?

Do not let the fact that you have to wear a standard uniform deflect you from the groundrules concerning your appearance. Whether you have to wear the uniform of an army officer or the white coat of a dental practitioner to make your presentation, you can still ensure that you create, and manage, your impact. In fact, the uniform might be an impactive part of the presentation. Important details here are shiny buttons and shoes, where relevant, and all-round perfect grooming of your hair, and, for women, your make-up.

Many complementary therapists, for example reflexologists, wear white coats or tabards, which obviously signal cleanliness to an audience. If you normally wear such a uniform, consider whether you look best in pure white or whether ivory better suits your skin's colouring.

Of course, another significant consideration will be whether or not you feel the wearing of the uniform is appropriate.

Do you look current?

There is a strong assumption in the business world that those people who present a positive self-image make the greatest contribution. An up-to-date look and confident air puts you firmly in this category. If you do not present yourself effectively, are you sure you are not conveying the impression of someone whose ideas are emerging as if from another decade, and whose business ethos has been left behind in a time warp? The subconscious message being received may be that your tired and dated appearance reflects tired and dated ideas.

Here are a few easy ways to check whether or not your look is current.

- When did you last change your hairstyle? If you can't remember, book a hairdresser's appointment now!
- For how long have you had your spectacles? Phone the optician today?
- Are you wearing a 1995 favourite band's touring T-shirt? Change it for a plain top.
- Are your accessories plastic? Change your briefcase/portfolio, watch, pen, to the best quality you can afford.

Do not confuse a current look with a high fashion look. The latter is welcomed largely only in the fashion industry itself and its related industries, and would not be welcomed in most other employment fields.

For men, the simplest check is to ask themselves how long they have been wearing the suit they intend to wear for the presentation. Old suits can frequently spoil the image you want to project. Women should, for example, check their hem lengths, the height and shape of their shoe heels, and certainly the width of their shoulder pads. 'Power dressing' started and finished in the 1980s.

- Be appropriately dressed
- Check out the dress code
- Pay attention to the details of your uniform or dress
- Bring your appearance up to date

Your behaviour

This topic is covered throughout the book, so there are only two reminders to be included here. Remember:

- your appearance can affect your performance
- confidence in your appearance gives you confidence in your presentation.

YES, BUT WHAT DO I WEAR?

Appropriate dress is more important than *what* dress, but whatever you decide on should achieve your aim of creating the most effective impact. Let's move on to your actual outfit.

- Deciding what to wear
- Focusing the audience's attention
- Being comfortable

When to decide what to wear

Many of you who are experienced presenters may well have a 'presenting outfit'. (Ask yourself how long you have been wearing it? Is it still current and appropriate?). Whether you are experienced or not, the time to decide what you are going to wear is not when you wake up on the morning of the presentation. Readers might recall a TV ad featuring a young man whose mother vetoed his yellow T-shirt and scrambled to wash his white shirt in time for an interview … the closing shots of his shirt-tail flapping outside his trousers reveal quite another image than the one he presented.

The earlier you decide what you are going to wear, the better, preferably when you are shopping for your clothes. You obviously can't buy an outfit for a presentation if you don't know that you are going to give one. But the idea of enhancing your personal image should always be behind your clothes shopping – you don't know when you might be called upon to be a presenter.

The latest time you can decide what you are going to wear is the evening before your presentation. Even if you have not given any thought before this, do it now. This gives you at least the opportunity to do many things that will ensure you are effectively presented on the following day – from pressing and mending clothes to polishing shoes and putting your accessories together.

How to focus the audience's attention

When you are making a presentation, except when you are using your visual aid, you want the audience to focus on your face. Because the eye is attracted to the lightest, brightest or most detailed aspect in its vision, in clothing terms, you should always keep the focal point of your outfit near your face.

Ensure your comfort

Your comfort during your presentation is of paramount importance to the success of your delivery – another good reason for not rushing out in the morning to buy something (anything) to wear. You won't, for instance, be able to tell whether the pair of shoes that were so comfortable in the shop will prove quite the opposite when you have had them on your feet for an hour.

You should be wearing clothes in which you are at ease, which are comfortable, and which allow you freedom of movement. Practise sitting down as if by an OHP, standing and addressing your 'audience' and taking a few steps towards one of your visual aids. Try gesturing to a flipchart or raising your arms as you might do in the presentation. It is better to hear the rending of garments during your rehearsal than at the actual event. At all costs avoid your garments appearing to be coming apart at the seams and ensure that nothing is showing that shouldn't be – vest, slip, underpants' top, etc.

COLOURS, STYLES AND MUCH MORE

You will maximize your potential in every situation by knowing what works for and against you in self-presentation. Your clothes should both complement your physical appearance and reflect your personality. To do this you should consider:

- Clothing colours
- Clothing styles
- The fit of your clothes
- Grooming
- Accessories
- Capsuling your wardrobe

Clothing colours

Colour is the most important element of an outfit, because the language of colour is universal. Colours have associations in people's minds (red for danger, green for peace, yellow for sunshine, blue for cold – the connotations are endless), and colour can usually be seen easily from a distance. You can and should use colour in your wardrobe to help create your impact, focus on you and as an expression of yourself.

In this context, think of the saying 'You are what you wear' and then think of what colours you are going to wear for your presentation. It is certainly the case that you can help lift your spirits (and those of your audience, especially if you are doing the post-lunch session) by wearing a positive colour. If you wear black from head to foot, how successful do you think you would be in lifting a solemn, judgemental mood you would impose on your audience of, say, student nurses? Conversely, are you beginning to realize that a khaki safari suit may be deemed both inappropriate and frivolous if your presentation is to your company's board of directors?

You can also use colour in your outfit as a kind of protective armour, disproving the theory that 'the external is the reflection of the internal'. This means that you present an effective image for your self-esteem that will carry you through the most difficult situations. Use colour in your clothing to project a positive mood and you will avoid falling victim to hiding behind a colour that does not complement your total image.

Which colours?

Wearing colours successfully means harmonizing the colour's dominant characteristics with those of your own natural colouring, taking into account your skin tone, eye and hair colour.

Characteristics in colour, as with our own colour pattern, fall into three categories, each with a distinctive pairing.

> ■ **Depth** – deep versus light
> ■ **Undertone** – cool versus warm
> ■ **Clarity** – bright versus muted

Depth. Here the intensity of a colour – light, medium or dark – is defined, where, on a scale of 0 to 10, black scores 0 (deep) and white scores 10 (light). The deep look projects strength as opposed to the softer, more delicate look of the light.

Undertone. The undertone defines whether a colour is blue-based (cool) or yellow-based (warm). Examples include fuschia pink (cool for people with a rosy tinge to their skin) and tomato red (warm for those who are more golden in skintone).

Clarity. A colour's clarity – brightness or muted quality – is defined by the amount of grey which has been added to its original brightness. Bright colours need matching brightness (for example, high contrast between the hair and skin colours) in the colour pattern of the wearer; muted colours are successfully worn by those with softer contrasts.

Not all colours, however, are suitable or acceptable for business situations, and you need to have a good grasp of the colours that you could (or should) and cannot (or should not) wear. For ease of recognition, clothing colours are most commonly divided into three groups.

- neutrals
- pastels
- accent colours.

Neutrals include black, navy, grey and possibly brown, and these colours should form the backbone of your business wardrobe. Garments in neutrals are your investment buys – you should spend as much on them as you can afford – and include suits, jackets, shoes and accessories. The neutral that works best for you will probably be nearest your hair or eye colours.

Pastels are the light colours you use to complement your neutrals, for example pale blue or ivory. Avoid wearing entire outfits in pale shades for a presentation, as you could appear diaphanous on stage.

Accent colours are where you can run (a little) riot. I was going to use the expression 'paint the town red', but you need to be wary of wearing red for a presentation. Colour psychologist Angela Wright has written that the colour red is the most impactful on the eye as it requires the most eye adjustment to register. Green on the other hand, requires the least eye adjustment and is therefore considered most restful on the eye.

It is your accent colours, worn in combination with your neutrals that allow you to fully express your personality. Here you can introduce pattern – polka dots, stripes, Liberty print, etc – whatever expresses you best.

You also need to consider the combination of colours you wear. The higher the contrast in your clothing (black and white being the most extreme contrast possible), the more authority you project. You need only think of the authority figures in our society – judges, the police – to understand how this idea works. High contrast clothing might be ideal for a large audience because you will be easily visible, but be aware that under some circumstances, too authoritative a look might well make you seem aloof and unapproachable.

If your presentation is to a smaller group, or a more informal one, blend your colours so that you indicate approachability. You might wear a grey suit with a peach shirt or blouse, and an eye-catching tie or scarf. Here too, if it would be appropriate, you may be able to move away from both your neutrals and the traditional suit into, say, dark green trousers or skirt and a sports jacket or cardigan.

A final word on the colour of your clothing. Try to find out what colour the background to your presentation will be, so that you can wear something that will contrast effectively. You do not want to run the risk of beginning your presentation and hearing the audience say 'We can't see you' because you have melted into the background.

Clothing shapes and styles

Many people are extremely anxious about their size, an expression usually which implies that they are 'carrying weight'. But anxiety can be experienced just as much by those who are petite or tall. We may have heard that designer samples rarely go above a size 10 and we probably know that a size 16 is hardly ever the same in any two high street chain stores – but we still worry. (It is, incidentally, much simpler for the male population – a chest measurement of 44 inches, a waist measurement of 38 inches and an inside leg measurement of 33 inches are, usually, the same wherever you shop.)

The size on the label of the garment you buy and your actual measurements are less important than the physical structure of your body. What is important is that you should match your clothing shapes and styles to the structure of your body. Men's and women's body shapes are different, but for both sexes, body shapes fall into three distinct categories.

For men:
■ the 'body builder' shape – broad shoulders tapering to slim hips
■ the 'straight' or Savile Row shape – shoulder width equalling that of the hips
■ the 'contoured' or rounded shape.

For women:
- the straight silhouette
- the curved silhouette
- the semi-straight silhouette.

The use of expressions such as straight, rounded and semi-straight are a good indication of how you can most successfully dress your individual body shape.

Whether male or female, if you have a 'straight' shape, with minimum curves, you should dress this shape with minimum curves. Your best look will consist of straight-cut garments which hang well from the shoulders and show off your best angles.

The more curved, or rounded your shape, the more you enhance this with a waisted, softer draping of fabric. For men, this might mean wearing a jacket with less pronounced lapels; women might successfully wear a wrap-around skirt.

It follows that if your shape falls somewhere between these two you can wear a combination of soft and straight shapes.

Presentation guidelines

Whatever your shape, when you are making a presentation also bear the following guidelines in mind.

Keep to simple lines and patterns or mixes of patterns. Having made your impact, keep the audience's concentration on your presentation, not whether your scarf or tie is the one they saw at a recent Royal Society exhibition or in the Tie Rack sale.

Keep your patterns to scale. If you are tall and large-boned then you can probably afford the dramatic gesture of a flamboyantly checked suit or a large-print scarf. This will also enable you to break up the potentially (literally) overpowering image you present. Both of these would dwarf a smaller individual who needs, rather, to miniaturize patterns. A shorter person should think in terms of slimming, and therefore lengthening lines – whether or not they are carrying weight.

Think about the texture of what you are wearing. In clothing, as in nature, light reflects and shadow recedes. So if you are wearing a shiny fabric, try to ensure that the lighting in the presentation room will not bounce off like light from a mirrored ball. Similarly, a heavily textured garment such as a tweed suit, especially if it is dark, may make you appear a woolly blur on stage.

The fit of your clothes. Whether or not you are a so-called 'standard' size, the good *fit* of your clothes is also essential – the size on the label is not important. Pockets should lie flat and not gape open; jackets should button with ease and not strain across the stomach; sleeves should show half an inch below your jacket cuff. Women should be able to turn their skirts round with ease, which means that they do not ride up when you sit down and, even worse, show the lining. Men should not show a glimpse of leg between the tops of their socks and the bottom of their trousers.

Anything ill-fitting, whether it is too tight or too big, will detract from your image and hence from your message.

Grooming

There is no substitute for good grooming, which in terms of self-presentation is the equivalent of the detailed preparation you spend on the other aspects of your presentation. Good grooming goes far beyond being the 'finishing touches' to your image, and in fact lies at the heart of effective self-presentation.

Start your grooming early by buying the best quality clothes you can afford – then you must look after them.

TEN TIPS FOR YOUR CLOTHES

1. Always hang your clothes up when you take them off, on good quality, separate hangers
2. Hang them outside your wardrobe overnight to air
3. Brush your clothes after wearing them and again before you go out
4. Empty all your pockets
5. Untie ties and scarves
6. Insert shoe trees as soon as you take them off
7. Check your clothes and shoes regularly and make minor repairs
8. Have your clothes cleaned regularly
9. Clean your shoes as soon as you can
10. Use proper clothes bags, not dry cleaners' plastic covers

---

Good grooming also, obviously, includes looking after yourself.

TEN TIPS FOR YOU

1. Ensure that you do not suffer from body odour – use a deodorant
2. Use your dentist and follow their advice
3. Have your hair cut regularly and in a style that suits you
4. Get rid of dandruff
5. Men should shave carefully every day or keep beards trimmed
6. Avoid clothing that distracts attention – eg ill-fitting or skimpy
7. Pay attention to your hands and nails – use a hand cream, have a manicure
8. Cleanse, tone and moisturize your face daily
9. Women should wear make-up particularly when stage lighting is in use
10. Avoid strong fragrances – they may not be everyone else's favourite and they linger on your clothes

---

Accessories

Accessories say as much about you and your self-image as the clothes you wear. Again, they should be the best quality you can afford and should be in scale with your size and shape. If you are of medium height and build, your clothing patterns and accessories should be to medium scale. A taller person can more successfully carry a large portfolio; someone smaller would be better advised to use a compact briefcase.

Keeping to your scale is not always possible if you are having to carry many visual aids yourself to the presentation. Once they are all in the room, however, you should follow the setting-up procedures described in Chapter 4 and then get rid of surplus boxes, carrier bags, papers, pens, etc. Put them all in a corner of the room or hide them under a cloth-covered table. But at all costs, as you begin your presentation avoid being surrounded by clutter – briefcase, handbag, diary, address book, business cards, etc.

Accessories enable you to personalize your outfit. By changing the buttons on a blazer or jacket or adding a silk handkerchief to your breast pocket you can turn a chainstore garment into one that more clearly and successfully expresses you.

Good accessories also have the ability to 'lift' an inexpensive garment, transforming it into one that looks tailor-made for you. For example, a luxurious silk tie or scarf will enhance any suit, although don't go over the top. Remember the reverse is also true – a simple cotton bandana will detract from the beautiful fabric, cut and fit of your designer jacket.

Capsuling

Having a 'capsule' wardrobe – a limited number of garments that work well together – is important in the business world, as it allows you to ring the changes with your investment buys in neutrals, perhaps adding pastels and accent colours according to the season's 'new' colours.

A capsule wardrobe is especially important if you are giving a series of presentations or presenting away from home. In the first case you may think it necessary to create a fresh impact every morning, but be careful that your audience does not spend your sessions wondering whether you have a trunkful of clothes hidden in your room. In both cases you may be taking many handouts, questionnaires, OHP slides of flipchart sheets. Imagine how much greater your carrying capacity for these would be if you did not have to carry a very extensive wardrobe in order to present yourself effectively for the week. A capsule wardrobe can answer many of your anguished personal appearance questions, from 'What shall I wear?' to 'Do I look all right?'

IN CONCLUSION

'No dress can be good which is not useful and adapted to practical necessities, nor can any dress be perfect into which the element of individuality does not enter'. (Mrs Oliphant, *Dress*, 1878)

Before you leave your home, office or hotel room for your presentation, try to look in a full-length mirror, and ask yourself three questions:

> - Is what I see a true reflection of me?
> - Do I like what I see?
> - Am I making a good impression on myself?

If your answer to all three is yes, then you know that you look good, you will feel good and you can make your presentation with confidence in the image you are presenting.

SOME ACTIVITIES TO CONSIDER

ACTIVITY: Think of any presentations you have attended. List all the personal presentation points about the presenters you can remember. What did you think of these presenters? Were their images effective ones? If so, why? If not, why not? How could they have improved themselves?

ACTIVITY: Think of what you wore at your last presentation. Were you satisfied with the image you presented? Write down what you wish you had worn. Would that have been possible?

ACTIVITY

1. Make a list of what you consider to be the positive and negative aspects of your image. Then say them out loud and note their effect on your self-esteem.
2. If you are performing this activity in a group, each member should write on a piece of paper the positive and negative aspects of the images of each other member of the group. These should then be distributed and discussed as appropriate. (Note: this second part of the activity should only be attempted with a group in which the individuals have spent some time with each other, are open with each other and have shown they can accept critical feedback.)

ACTIVITY: Make a list of the neutrals, pastels and accent colours in your wardrobe. Now try to mix and match them into a capsule wardrobe for business.

ACTIVITY: There are a number of videos available that, in addition to containing material for the subject relevant to the video, also demonstrate a presenter in action (some of these videos are included in the 'Recommended Reading' section at the end of this book) so other presenter styles can be observed. View some of these different videos and:

1. Identify and analyse the (a) construction of the presentation, and (b) the presentation techniques exhibited
2. Discuss and evaluate what has been identified and analysed
3. Discuss the presentations in relation to (a) your style and (b) to what extent you would wish to reflect these other styles in that of your own.

(If time is available, it would then be valuable to arrange a series of brief presentations to enable the learner-presenters to practise their action proposals.)

8

—

On Stage – At the Start

This chapter:

■ Offers hints, tips and guidance on techniques for the effective
  delivery of the presentation:
  - before the presentation starts
  - opening the presentation

TECHNIQUES TO USE BEFORE YOU START

There may be occasions when you will have some time before the start
of the presentation and the appearance of the audience – if so, make
full use of this luxury as it might make all the difference in the delivery
of your presentation. Some positive actions that can be taken include:

■ Stand 'on stage' and breathe in the atmosphere of the environment
■ Identify where you are going to stand or sit and where you will move
  during the presentation
■ Can you see all of the audience?
■ Can all the audience see you?
■ Check your brief and place it in the most appropriate spot
■ Check your visual aids
■ Check the equipment and its operation
■ Can all the audience see and read the visual aids?
■ Try to be in your place before the audience arrives

Stand 'on stage' and breathe in the atmosphere of the environment

Just standing where you will be speaking and taking in the room or auditorium will give you a sense of what it will be like when you are giving your presentation. You may have been told that it is a large/ medium/small room, or its approximate dimensions, but this information will probably have meant little to you. The size is brought home clearly when you see it from 'on stage' and this can help to increase your confidence – much more so than if you had to walk straight in and start speaking immediately without any knowledge of the environment.

Identify where you are going to stand or sit and where you will move during the presentation

You may have been provided with a lectern – are you going to use it? If not, what is the alternative? If there are any changes to be made, see the organizer immediately. Do you want or do you have to move around during the presentation, either because that is your manner or you have to move over to a visual aid? Practise these moves and ensure that there are no cables or other obstacles over which you could trip.

Can you see all of the audience?

Provided the audience is not so large that the last row fades into the distance, you will want to have a clear sight of everyone present so that you can judge reactions. If, standing 'on stage' before the event, you see that this overall sight will be interfered with, you have time to modify your position or even move some of the seats.

Can all the audience see you?

Much of your message will get across to the audience if they can see you, rather than only be able to hear you – in which case you might just as well give them a tape recorder and a tape of your talk! So much is added to the presentation by the audience's sight and reaction to your physical manner and approach.

Check your brief and place it in the most appropriate spot

This will depend on the furniture in the area from which you will be speaking. If you have to speak from a lectern, your brief goes there; if you are to sit at a desk or table, check the chair position and place the brief accordingly; if you are to stand, ensure that your brief is written on index cards that are tagged together. In some circumstances you will be moving around quite a lot, so you will need to ensure that there is a desk or table placed strategically on which you can have your brief ready for use as necessary.

Check your visual aids

If some time has passed between the production of your aids and the actual event, a variety of changes or accidents can occur. The inform-ation that was current when you completed the aid may have changed in the interim period; flipchart sheets might have been torn or smudged or, when you see the size of the room, their size or use is incorrect; OHP slides can become out of date, smudged or lose part of the lettering etc.

Check the equipment and its operation

There can be few worse experiences for a presenter, particularly one who is already very nervous, to switch on an audiovisual aid, OHP or large projector, only to find that it doesn't work. In some cases this may simply be due to the apparatus not being plugged into the socket or the socket not being switched on. But there could have been an equipment failure of a more serious nature. Pre-event checks should establish this, although there is no guarantee that there will not be some failure between checking and switching on 'for real'. We can only hope that Murphy has gone away on holiday!

Can all the audience see and read the visual aids?

You will certainly have spent a substantial time in designing and preparing your visual or audiovisual aids and you will intend to use them for maximum effect. Much of this effect will be lost if part of your audience cannot see them or read some of them. Will the last row of the audience be too far away to see them clearly? Will the edges of the audience area be at too acute an angle for the images to be seen? As mentioned earlier, the only way to ensure success is to go into the auditorium's seating area and check whether you can see all that needs to be seen.

Try to be in your place before the audience arrives

Walk into a room or hall full of people and the potential audience can become a frightening sea of anonymous, or worse, antagonistic faces. Even a small group can create a sense of unease as they will all be looking at *you*. If, however, you are already there when the audience starts to enter, you are looking at *them*, probably in small groups or as individuals, and perhaps assessing their interest or activity level, etc. If, however, you are required to walk into an existing group, once in the room, stop and look around at them – even if you don't really *see* them this apparent contact will create a feeling in the audience that you are interested in them. But don't stand too long looking as this might be interpreted that you have been rooted to the spot with fear!

JUST BEFORE YOU GO 'ON STAGE'

- If possible, go outside for some fresh air
- Breathe this fresh air deeply and slowly
- Pay a final visit to the cloakroom
- Check your dress
- Return to the presentation room looking forward to the presentation

IMMEDIATELY BEFORE STARTING TO SPEAK

- Accept that you are going to feel nervous
- Look at the audience
- Remember they are only people like you
- Remember all your planning and preparation
- Tell yourself that you are going to stand up
  and help them learn and enjoy your presentation, and that you are going
  to enjoy it too
- Have a sip of water
- Try not to look nervous
- Don't fiddle with your clothing
- Leave your notes alone
- Don't have a pen or pencil in your hand
- You know you are not going to give a 100 per cent perfect presentation –
  nobody ever does – but you know that you should be comfortable enough
  to make it effective
- (Offer a little prayer)

- Accept that you are going to feel nervous. Very few people avoid this, and it actually helps you to be ready to give a good presentation. There are some people, however, who find it difficult to overcome this nervousness – unless they can eventually overcome it, or are the only person who can present the material (which is unlikely), they will be best advised not to be the presenter.

- Look at the audience and let them see you looking at them rather than at the floor in front of you. Remember that non-verbal signals are quickly recognized, and this sign of unease may not encourage them to help you.

- Remember they are only people like you, probably not as well informed and possibly people who have been through the distress of presenting themselves.

- Remember all your planning and preparation, but do not let it become a worry.

- Tell yourself that you are going to stand up and help them learn and enjoy your presentation, and that you are going to enjoy it too.

- Have a sip of water to lubricate your throat. Avoid alcohol – even if vodka has the same appearance as water – as you may be tempted to take too much, becoming more incoherent as the presentation proceeds.

■ Try not to look nervous (even if all is panic inside). Don't fiddle with your tie, cuffs, dress, hair, fingers (put them on your knees in front of you – except when you're clenching them). Leave your notes alone and don't have a pen or pencil in your hand (you will surely fiddle with it, or even worse, drop it).

■ You know you are not going to give a 100 percent perfect presentation – *nobody* ever does – but you know that you should be comfortable enough to make it effective.

■ (Offer a little prayer – who knows, it may help you!)

STARTING YOUR PRESENTATION

It is at this point, just before starting to speak, that the stage fright, butterflies or fear of presentations can either appear or increase. We saw in Chapter 1 that one of the principal reasons for this fear is not the presentation itself, but the fear of making a fool of oneself. In the sections following this the emphasis was on knowing what is facing you, and planning as effectively as you can. This planning and preparation will help you to face the audience with much more confidence than otherwise and with the awareness of being in control. The factors we identified earlier will help somewhat to calm the butterflies in that:

■ the audience knows less than the presenter about the subject (this is almost always the case);

■ the audience wants to know about the subject (this is almost always the case);

■ the presenter knows the subject to be presented (effective preparation will have ensured this);

■ the best way of presenting it has been identified (there is a variety of techniques from which to choose);

■ the presentation will be interesting (you know that your material is interesting so how you personally present it will control the audience's interest);

■ the presenter is in the position of power to control the presentation and hence, to some extent, its success (even if the audience is senior in status and power, the presenter is the one in front and in charge of the presentation).

But, whatever is done in all these respects, unless you are over-confident or unfeeling for the audience as people, as soon as you enter the presentation area or you stand up to start talking, the butterflies will appear. In fact they will almost certainly arrive before this – for example walking into the presentation room, waiting to be introduced. It is doubtful whether this initial feeling will ever be conquered, however experienced the presenter becomes – there is no absolute inverse ratio to the number of butterflies with the number of presentations given. The more experience you gain, the greater the possibility of fewer butterflies, but this is not guaranteed. Of course there are natural speakers who never suffer, but they are few.

CONTROLLING THE BUTTERFLIES

The introductions have been made and you stand up to speak – and what happens? The mouth dries up, the heart starts pounding (or pounds even harder than it did a few moments ago), the knees and hands start trembling, and the dreaded butterflies perform a ballet in the stomach.

Remember that the audience will also be experiencing some emotion, although not as extreme as the presenter. They may not know the presenter and be suspicious about what he or she is going to say, how they are going to say it and whether it will be worth listening to. Is it going to be worth their while spending time at the presentation and will they learn something from the experience, in addition to enjoying it? There may be silent thoughts – 'Oh no, not somebody else I have to sit and listen to', 'These chairs are hard', 'I wish somebody would turn up/down the heating', and so on. But being aware of this is no consolation to you at this point.

GETTING STARTED

Here are one or two suggestions to help you get started.

- ■ Accept the butterfly effects, take advantage of them and get going
- ■ Take slower, deeper breaths than normal
- ■ Clench and unclench your fists (out of sight)
- ■ Stand up to start and to introduce yourself and the subject; then sit down
- ■ Talk more slowly than you normally do
- ■ Start with the simple things
- ■ If there is a lectern stay behind it for the first few seconds, then get away from it
- ■ Don't sit behind a table or *on* it

- The adrenaline will flow, giving you the extra energy you need but also producing the stage fright effects – accept that this is happening, take advantage of it and get going.

- Relax as much as you can and take slower, deeper breaths than normal or clench and unclench your fists (ensure that the audience doesn't see you – they might interpret this as aggression).

- Even if you are going to sit for the presentation, stand up to start and to introduce yourself and the subject; then sit down.

- Talk more slowly than you normally do – in fact, if you didn't do this you would talk much faster than normal, even gabble, so slowing down to what you think is below your normal speed will probably make the pace about right. Nervousness shows itself in accelerated talking and usually signals clearly that you are nervous – don't let the audience know this!

- Start with the simple things, such as who you are and what you are going to talk about – unless you are very experienced it is dangerous to try something too complicated or adventurous at this very early stage.

- If there is a lectern stay behind it for the first few seconds, then get away from it; it is a barrier between you and the audience. This may be unavoidable however, because, for example, the microphone is fixed there (an alternative could be a lapel/tie/neck radio or long cordmike). Similarly if you have been placed behind a table, try to work out some way of getting to the side or in front of it – sitting on the table is not always a good idea as you will tend to swing your legs. Move your chair to the side – you are passing a message to the audience that you don't want this barrier between you. Lecterns and tables are principally repositories for your notes and visual aids.

SOME SPECIFIC TECHNIQUES TO USE WHEN OPENING THE PRESENTATION

- Have written down the first sentence or two you are going to say
- Be sure of your introduction and how to make it
- Don't apologize
- Grab their attention – start with a 'bang'
- After your introduction, pause to encourage attention
- Describe the framework of the talk
- Tell them what you're going to tell them
- Define the questioning strategy
- Set the mood – use humour, ask a question
- Try to start with agreement

Your opening sentences

A technique almost guaranteed to increase your confidence at the start is knowing exactly what you are going to say to get you going. You may think that, having thought about it and knowing what you want to say, you will say it – beware, your head may empty of everything as soon as you open your mouth. By all means memorize your first sentence or two, but also have them written down on a separate piece of paper that you will have directly in front of you. You will never then be at a loss for what you are going to say at the starting point.

This tip may be most relevant when you are being introduced by someone else – when they stop speaking, you have to start. If you are introducing yourself you have a variety of ways of doing this and you can control when you actually start speaking.

Introductions

Are you going to be introduced by somebody or will you have to do this yourself? If the former case, a brief note about yourself will help them, as they may have the same problems of knowing what they are going to say.

If you have to introduce yourself make sure that you know, before you attend the event, exactly what you want to say and how you are going to say it. Self-introductions should be as short as possible and should try to satisfy the audience who you are and of your credibility and authority to speak. This will create a balance between ensuring that you present your credentials but do not appear too autocratic, too dogmatic, too bigheaded or too shy. If you have had relevant material published, say so; but if you are a recognized author mentioning your books at the start may antagonize some people – it you must mention them, leave it to the end. It can be useful to mention them in a humorous way – in this way the impact may not be over the top.

Why should so much be made of the start of the presentation? Because this is the time when you are likely to be at your most nervous, and anything that will help you over these first few minutes can only do you good. Remember that the first ten seconds or so is used by the audience in forming a first impression of you as presenter. The next two minutes or so will be used as confirmation of that first impression – there is no second chance to make a first impression although it can be modified later, but even then the audience still holds fairly firmly to their first impression.

A different approach is to use a visual aid for your self-introduction – an OHP slide showing your name, organization, qualifications etc. However, be careful with this one as the audience may see it as gimmicky. Also, if you use such an aid, make sure everybody can see and read it. But whatever happens, don't read it out word for word.

Apologies

Do not start talking with an apologetic manner (although avoid an overbearing or patronizing approach) and, unless absolutely essential, avoid at this stage apologizing for anything. The more you apologize, the less will be your credibility. Why are you apologizing? It should certainly not be for the subject of the presentation or why you are giving it. Your aids should have been well prepared, so there will be no need for apology here – and your pre-talk checks help to avoid any reason for this. Never apologize for lack of time in preparation – you will not receive any sympathy from the audience, who may well feel insulted by your apparent lack of concern for them. Start on a positive note.

Grab their attention

Ninety per cent of the success of your presentation will be the result of your catching the audience's attention at or close to the start, and maintaining this attention. Comments are made above about introductions – either by yourself or another – and the need to keep these short. After these, the presentation proper starts. To make an impact start with a 'bang', not a whimper.

A 'bang' makes an impact and draws your audience's attention – knowing your audience will guide you to the extent of the 'bang'. You may not have to be revolutionary at the start as they may not be ready for it, they may resent it, may look on it as patronizing or see it as too gimmicky. However, experience shows that an impactive opening gives the presenter a greater chance of maintaining attention. The following suggest some ways of opening positively.

Pause

This advice links with the earlier comments suggesting that you slow down the speed of your delivery, particularly right at the start. After any necessary introduction do not go straight into the body of your talk. It is a difficult to explain the anomaly with audiences that although they want you to 'get on with it' they still prefer to be *introduced* to the subject. A deliberate pause after the introduction tells the audience that the introduction is complete and you will soon be starting the actual presentation. It is difficult to give guidance on how long this pause should be – a balance has to be struck between too short a pause (you will always think that it is longer than it really is), and one that is too long and makes the audience restless. Only experience will help you to strike this balance.

The framework of the talk

The success of a presentation will be helped by giving the audience an outline or map of what lies ahead in the time you have with them. Describe *briefly* the stages you will be following through the talk, and if you are going to use any particularly interesting or different aids. Define the questioning procedure – should questions be raised as they occur, or should they be kept to the end of the presentation, and what time will be allowed for this. If there is to be a summary handout, tell the audience this, so that there will be no need for them to take notes unless they wish to do so.

Tell them what you're going to tell them

One approach advises a three-stage technique for effective present-ations in which you should 'Tell 'em what you are going to tell 'em; Tell 'em; Tell 'em what you've told 'em'. In other words you start the presentation with a summary of the talk, then proceed with the main body of the talk, and at the end give a summary. This approach not only helps the audience but, particularly in the first 'Tell 'em', you refresh your mind about the task ahead.

A useful approach here is to use a sales technique and to let the audience know, not the features of the presentation, but the benefits to them from the talk – of course you need to ensure that it is the type of presentation that *will* achieve some benefits for them!

The questioning strategy

This has been commented on above in the context of letting the audience know at the start what the questioning strategy will be. The alternatives are to accept questions during the presentation, as they arise, or to have the audience hold questions until the end of the talk. Only if you have unlimited time and are secure in the knowledge that the audience will 'stay with you' should you allow interruptive questions. These can cause chaos with a closely timed presentation, so in most cases you will be advising the audience that time will be allowed at the end for questions. *Make sure that you do in fact build in time for this.*

Set the mood

The mood for the presentation will be largely set at this early stage, principally by the way you approach the subject as you introduce it. A serious topic will need to be dealt with in a serious manner, and a very lighthearted start would be inappropriate. A start that contains elements of humour will indicate to the audience that your presentation will not be too 'heavy' (see below for more guidance on humour). If you start and keep on talking, this will indicate to the audience that the presentation will be principally led by you. If, at an early stage, you involve the audience – ask *them* a question, give them an exercise, put them into buzz groups etc – you will be indicating that this is how you intend to continue and you *want* them to be involved. Of course, the mood of the start will not necessarily have to be maintained throughout the presentation and, as suggested earlier, interesting and effective presentations include a number of approaches, techniques and events.

Try to start with agreement

Within your presentation plan and objectives, try to start with a topic with which the audience will agree. Their receptivity is much greater if you start them nodding in agreement. Some presenters can get away with a conflict or a disagreement at the start, with the intention of encouraging the audience to be interested and reactive, but for most presenters the dangers are too great to take the chance of antagonizing the audience from the start.

SOME SPECIFIC TYPES OF OPENER

- Use a short, relevant, understandable quotation
- Try humour – use with care
- Ask a question
- Try to make personal visual impact
- Use a topical reference
- Employ shock tactics – be ready to duck!
- Use an icebreaker
- Try a buzz group
- Use an expectations chart

Quotations

Some presenters, particularly where the subject and the approach are academic, like to start the presentation with a quotation. The guidelines for using these include:

- keep them short;
- make the quotation relevant and appropriate to the subject;
- ensure that the audience will understand them and that they relate to the subject;
- ensure that the audience will understand the importance of the originator of the quote and who they are – quotes by the Chief Executive, for example, will carry more weight with an organization's employees than one by Wittgenstein (however profound).

Unless the quotation contains only one or two words, it is more likely to satisfy the criteria described above if it is exhibited on a visual aid, eg an OHP slide.

Humour

There are two principal forms of humour that can be used by a presenter. Some presenters have an instinctive and unconscious humorous manner that defies an accurate description and definition. Certainly it is very difficult, if not impossible, to copy and it is dangerous to try. These 'humorists' cannot help themselves, even in the most serious situations, and it is here that the danger lies for them.

The other humour is deliberate and has its own difficulties and dangers. This humour, at the start of a presentation, usually consists of the presenter telling a joke. Beware! It is very dangerous simply to tell a joke just to get a laugh or with the intention of lightening the atmosphere.

- Will the audience understand the joke?
- Will they find it funny?
- Will they think 'What has that got to do with anything?'
- Might it offend on grounds of race, colour, religion, disability, sex?
- Can you actually tell jokes effectively?

As far as the last point is concerned, many people are unable to carry off a joke. If you are one of these, forget it, as a failed joke will do more harm than none at all.

If you must tell a joke, make it relevant and appropriate, one that is directly related to the subject, eg an anecdote about what happened to you in the situation to be discussed.

Question at start

It was suggested earlier that a question at the start might be a useful approach to take. This serves a number of purposes.

- It gives you something to say to start the presentation!
- It lets the audience know that you want to involve them.
- A question suggests to the audience that the event is going to be interactive (and fun?).
- It tells the audience that you are interested in communicating with them, rather than just lecturing *at* them.

Typical questions can include ones as simple as 'Can you hear me at the back?' or 'Can anybody not see the visual aids?' (This is a more effective way of finding out this information than asking if everybody can see them.) But other questions might relate to the extent of the knowledge or experience of the subject within the audience, or the extent to which the audience want to progress in the subject. Unless you have almost unrestricted time, ask questions that entail short-answer or even yes/no responses – even in the latter case the audience will feel it is being involved if the questioning is handled carefully and not developed into a staccato inquisition.

Visual impact

The usual advice about the visual impact you should try to achieve revolves around 'be yourself'. This is excellent if you are naturally an enthusiastic, motivated, charismatic, personable person whom everybody likes on sight. But many of us are none of these, and to create some impact we must pretend in some way or force a particular manner. However, this acting (for that is what many presenters have to achieve) must not be so extreme and obviously out of character that the audience realizes this pretence and reacts against it.

Even if you are not usually enthusiastic, it normally does not require much to be enthusiastic about the topic and show your enthusiasm; you could, for example, try to talk with more sparkle in your voice than usual. This is all that is normally required. Unless the situation demands it, do not go over the top by putting on an act that will get in the way of rather than support the presentation.

So the general advice is: be yourself as far as this is relevant, but also ensure that you send signals to the audience that you care for them and the subject and you want to help them.

Topical reference

A natural and usually successful starting point is to relate the presentation to a current situation or series of events – 'My talk is particularly relevant today, as listening to the early news this morning it was reported that . . .' You must ensure that it *is* relevant, otherwise you suffer a drop in credibility right at the start.

Shock tactics

A feasible opening gambit, although potentially one of the most dangerous, is to use some form of shock tactic. This might be a fact that is intended to shock and so try to make the audience realize the importance of the subject. For example, in a presentation about the effects of war a statement intended to shock might be that in Angola there are at least 70,000 people who have lost one or more limbs through stepping on abandoned land mines. The verbal statement could be supported by a projected graphic showing the number, or perhaps the number in large lettering superimposed on an image of limbless cases.

An alternative is to make a provocative or contentious statement – this is probably the most dangerous of all as the audience might turn against you, however you explain the reason for your statement. If you control the amount of contention so that the audience's feathers are only slightly ruffled, and you immediately follow up the statement with a simple explanation, the risk is less.

One of the most shocking openings I have encountered, albeit highly effective, is a small but totally unexpected explosion at the back of the room shortly after the start of a presentation on explosives and their use in terrorist activities. Fortunately nobody had a bad heart. Because the amount of explosive was small, yet with a result beyond what might have been expected, the impact was so much greater.

A less frightening but equally dramatic example was at the start of a session on the unemployment benefit procedures relating to share fishermen – a potentially boring session – with the speaker arriving slightly late. He burst into the room wearing oilskins, sou'wester, and wellingtons, carrying a fishing rod complete with plastic fish. A colleague in the corridor threw a cupful of water at him as he announced that he had come to talk about share fishermen! It certainly started the event in a different way!

Icebreakers

Icebreakers are short activities that are used to ease the start of an event, to demonstrate interactivity and show the intention of having an interactive presentation. This encourages audience participation.

A different form of audience introduction can be a useful icebreaker. The presentation might be the first in a series of linked events and breaking the ice at the start of the first one can have a beneficial effect throughout the series.

There are hundreds of icebreaker introduction activities for both small and large audiences. One which is usually very effective for a large or medium sized audience is to ask everybody to stand up and talk to two other people whom they do not know for two minutes each. If you control the time this activity takes no longer than about five minutes. The noise can be deafening, but everybody has a lot of fun (especially if the activity is unexpected) and the atmosphere when everybody resumes their seats is completely different from five or six minutes earlier, and probably much more conducive to acceptance of the presentation.

Buzz groups can be useful icebreakers. The presenter might ask the audience to consider and comment on an opening statement. If this is done directly to the audience as a whole there can be a very embarrassing silence, or comments from only a small number of people. Using buzz groups, the audience is asked to form into small groups of, say, six to ten depending on the size of the audience, either by physically moving their seats into a group, or by grouping with their neighbours and turning their seats to face the people behind them. The groups are given a period of time to discuss the statement and one of the group acts as recorder and eventually as reporter for the group. At the end of the period, the reporters are asked to comment on the results of their buzz group, the views being recorded on a flipchart or an OHP acetate sheet.

Again, the buzz groups generate a lot of noise that has the effect of making the situation more informal; the audience gets to know some of their peers somewhat; interactivity is introduced and the presenter discovers a lot of information about the views of the audience. The use of reporters ensures that comments are easily forthcoming as these people are not having to present personal views in front of a group.

The use of buzz groups has the secondary, but very welcome result of giving the presenter time to settle down to the atmosphere of the audience, knowing that there are going to be some immediate reactions.

Expectations chart

An expectations chart can be relevant and effective when the presentation:

- is extensive, ie one requiring a substantial period of time;
- is very much a learning situation;
- may be the first event in a consecutive series;

- is to be given to a group with whom the presenter has had no previous contact and does not know about their experience, skills or knowledge.

The use of this technique is very time consuming, not only in the time the individuals take in preparing their own chart, but in any discussion about the results of the group activity – for example, a statement or promise by the presenter about which expectations will be satisfied by the end of the event. In addition, it will be necessary to leave some time at the end of the presentation to assess the satisfaction of the group's expectations and offer guidance on what to do about the unsatisfied needs.

In practice, individuals are given a sheet – see Figure 8.1 – on which they are asked to record their hopes for the event and also their fears or concerns about it. These are written up on a visual aid – for example, a large flipchart sheet or poster – and, following discussion of some of the more unusual items, this poster is placed visibly on the wall, and referred to at the end.

EXPECTATIONS CHART	
Hopes/needs for and from the event	**Concerns/fears about the event**

Figure 8.1 *An expectations chart*

Whichever technique or activity you use as an opener, consider it carefully in your planning as some of the activities can eat into the time you have available. If you have only limited time, you may have to forgo a substantial opener, moving into the talk quickly – although even then you can use some of the above suggestions with effect. It is all too easy to become involved with complicated openers, only to discover that you have insufficient time to put over the essential message of your presentation. But, if you have the practical skills, if you find a relevant opener activity, and if you have sufficient time, their use can be significant.

WHAT TO SAY AND WHAT NOT TO SAY AT THE START

Let us complete the guidance for this starting stage of the presentation by considering some of the actual words to use and those not to use. Many presentations are ruined at the start by what the speaker says then and how they say it. Saying 'Unaccustomed as I am to public speaking' is an age-old starter that I still hear from time to time, but there are other gambits to avoid. These include:

- 'I have been told to come and speak to you about . . .' (this will be seen as a lack of interest because you have been forced to speak).
- 'I have been told to stand up, speak up and sit down' (they will be expecting you to do that and you should do it).
- 'I'm going to tell you what I'm going to tell you, etc' (this will come across as patronizing – just do it).
- 'I'm sure you know more about . . . than I do' (the immediate audience reaction will be to wonder why you are there at all).
- 'I just want to say a few words' (this is usually followed by a long and boring monologue – only say this if you really have only a few words to say).
- 'I'd like to tell you a good story you may not have heard before' (it may not be a good story, they may have heard it before – and told better – and it sounds too much like someone else's catchphrase). If you know you have a good story – preferably original – tell it.

PRESENTATION TIMING

Timing is an important aspect of any presentation and reference has already been made to the use of time. The time element has three important factors:

- the timing of the whole presentation and the allocation of units of time within this;
- time control during the presentation;
- dealing with time wasters.

Organizing the timing of the presentation and the use of time during the presentation is difficult, and something that even experienced presenters find hard to get right every time. This aspect and that of dealing with time wasters is discussed in the next chapter.

What you may have to do at the start of the presentation is deal with members of the audience who arrive late. The concerned presenter would like to ensure that everyone in the audience hears everything that is being said, and may consider summarizing what has been said for the benefit of latecomers, especially if there is a group of them. There is simple advice for this – *Don't do it.*

If you do, you are using time for which you will have made no provision; you are singling this group out as important, which may be seen by those who arrived on time as an insult; catching up with what has happened is not your problem. This applies even when dealing with small groups, although in these situations you might acknowledge their late arrival (but obviously not sarcastically). You may, of course, have to take into account the status of the latecomers – you would probably wish to modify your approach if the latecomer was your Chief Executive! But the general guidance is to ignore latecomers and continue with the ones who had the good manners to ensure that they arrived on time.

One final comment here about time is that you should mention in your introduction of the presentation:

- the time at which (or after what period) the presentation will finish;
- the time reserved – 5, 10, 15 minutes – at the end for questions and discussion.

SOME ACTIVITIES TO CONSIDER

ACTIVITY Think of presentations you have attended and try to remember how they were started by the presenter. What effect did these methods have on you and to what extent did it affect your concentration etc on the presentation?

ACTIVITY

1. Consider and list as many ways you can think of that might reduce the pressures and their effects on you before you stand up to speak.
2. Consider and list as many ways you can think of that might reduce the pressures and their effects when actually starting the presentation.

ACTIVITY   Consider presentations or other events that you have attended and at which icebreakers were used. Discuss with the remainder of the group such aspects as:

- What was the nature of these?
- What did you learn from them?
- What was your opinion of those particular activities?
- Would you have used that icebreaker?
- Would you have used any icebreaker?

ACTIVITY

(a)   Divide the full group into smaller groups and ask each group to design an icebreaker that can be performed by the numbers in the small groups, preferably one appropriate to the current situation.

(b)   Each small group should have one other group perform their constructed icebreaker, followed by a discussion on the effectiveness of the icebreakers and their use in general.

ACTIVITY

1.   Consider and list any opening gambits you can recall being used by presenters whose presentations you have attended. What did you think of them?

2.   Consider and list any ideas you have about what sorts of things you should *not* say when starting your presentation.

3.   Consider and list some ideas you might say to make an effective start to your presentation.

9

On Stage – During and at the End
of the Event

This chapter:

■ offers hints, tips and guidance on techniques for the effective
  delivery of the presentation
    - during the event
    - at the end of the event
■ provides some guidelines to improve personal presentation.

GETTING YOUR MESSAGE ACROSS

Once you have started your presentation, a number of factors combine
to ensure success or otherwise. These include:

> ■ Where to look and how to stand
> ■ Making your case
> ■ Using your voice
> ■ Having an effective questioning strategy
> ■ Ending your presentation effectively

WHERE TO LOOK AND HOW TO STAND

Looking

- **Noticing a friendly face in the audience** at the start can help boost your confidence and you will be tempted to look at them often. After a while this could embarrass them with the thought 'Why does he/she always look at me?!' By all means start your presentation addressed to them, but quickly move your gaze away to other members of the audience.

- A useful technique is to **practise the 'lighthouse' look**. During the presentation, sweep your gaze across the audience, slowly – this will give each member the impression that they are being looked at. Don't sweep without stopping, do so at intervals, but don't exceed two or three seconds on each person. Watch out for the people at the extreme front of the seating arrangement; they are the ones most likely to be forgotten. This is particularly the case when the audience is in a 'U' shape and the ends of the U are almost in line with the speaker – it becomes almost a physical impossibility to look at these places.

- **Avoid looking above the heads of the audience**, perhaps at a clock at the back of the room. The audience will notice this and start to wonder why they are being avoided and think there is more interest in the time than in them.

- **Make sure an accurate clock or watch is available and easily visible** – do not rely on there being one in the presentation room, and certainly not one that can be clearly seen. A pocket watch with a clear face and hands is the most appropriate. Lay it on the desk beside the brief and develop the habit of glancing at it every now and then, without making this obvious. If your glance is followed by one or two members of the audience looking at their watches, it has been too obvious. 'Bleeping' watches are definitely out as they are not only disconcerting, but annoy many people.

- The friendly face in the audience
- Be a 'lighthouse'
- Look at the audience
- Ensure clock is visible

Sitting or standing

- It is frequently a personal preference whether you sit or stand. **If you do sit, this must not be *behind* a desk.** Pull the chair to one side of the desk if at all possible so that you avoid the desk being a barrier between you and the audience. It was suggested earlier that it may help your confidence if you sit at the beginning of your presentation, then get up as naturally as you can, for example, moving over to a flipchart. Unless the occasion is *very* informal, do not sit on the corner of the desk – inevitably you will swing your legs and distract the audience's attention.
- **Sitting with an OHP beside the speaker** is very convenient with a small group, although the OHP can be operated from a standing position. If a very large group is being addressed standing is usually necessary to allow the speaker to be both seen and heard. In such cases, ensure that when you have to use the OHP you are close to it and not at the opposite end of the 'stage', having to walk across, perhaps in silence.
- **When sitting down, relax and do not clench the arms of the chair.** Put your arms, hands, legs and feet where they are most comfortable. At one time presenters were told to sit upright in a chair – with their hands folded across their laps or placed, palms down, on their upper leg – and not to move around, but this is obviously too restricting for most people. As long as whatever you do does not distract your audience, sit in the most comfortable position for you. However, it is only too easy to slouch in the chair and thus give a poor impression of your attitude to the presentation. Move your bottom as far back in the chair as you can and sit up reasonably straight.
- **Circumstances may dictate that you have a lectern behind which you stand.** However, it is rare that this will be enforced and, if possible, you should move from behind it as soon as you are able. A lectern is of course very useful to hold your notes, a computer mouse etc, but move away from it as frequently as you can.
- **Do not stand rooted to one spot and sway as you talk.** Again, be natural and move around. But not too much – you do not want the audience to expend their energy following you around a platform for the duration of your talk.
- **Direction of movement.** The direction in which you move relative to the audience tends to suggest emphasis and direction of thought. If you move *forwards*, towards the audience, this suggests that what you are saying or are going to say is important, and you are emphasizing this fact.

Taking a step or two *backwards*, away from the audience, suggests that you have concluded a particular point and are giving them time to consider what you have said.

Moving across the 'stage' in a *sideways* direction can suggest that you are getting ready to start another point in your presentation – this may be strengthened by a preceding step or two backwards.

■ **Standing helps the continuity if both an OHP and flipchart or whiteboard are being used.** Moving from one to the other helps to break the permanent position in a natural way.

■ One of your pre-presentation acts should be to **check with the event organizer** what the environment is like and whether you will be expected to stand or sit, be near a desk, table or lectern, and whether it will be possible for you to move about. As far as possible, demand the arrangements that will suit *you* most as this will help your confidence.

■ **Follow a common-sense approach and do not be over-restricted by the 'rules'** – your actions should be aimed at making your position comfortable and helping your audience appreciate your presentation.

THE MAIN PART OF THE PRESENTATION

It is obviously most effective to move into the main part of the presentation as soon as possible, particularly when time is limited. In the pre-event preparation the key points to make will have been identified, the Must, Should and Could Knows noted, and time allocated to each of the points. Now is the time to deliver this material in as clear, articulate and logical manner as possible. To what extent the message gets across will depend on the material and its present-ation. A considerable amount of the presentation impact will depend on how you as the presenter come across to your audience. This will be determined by both verbal and non-verbal approaches.

Making your case

The major part of your presentation will be concerned with stating the case. A useful, logical and clear structure has been found to be:

1. State your information, view or proposition
2. Show evidence and proof to support these, including counters to opposition arguments that you have already anticipated
3. Repeat the information, view or proposition in a summarized form
4. Seek questions, view, agreement etc from the audience
5. Review the discussion and summarize the results
6. Review the presentation and summarize the key points.

Although this has been described as a structure, and some people react against a structured approach, it is really one of common sense rather than a forced, rigid discipline.

Perhaps rather more disciplined is the manner in which the material will be presented. Naturally it will be in a logical manner, but which is the most effective or appropriate logical manner? This will depend to a large extent on the complexity of the material, the existing knowledge of the audience, the presentation objectives and the time available.

The sequencing of your material was considered in the preparation stage and alternatives were offered.

- Move from the *known* to the *unknown*
- Develop the *simple* to the *complex*
- Progress from the *easy* to the *difficult*
- Use a logical stepping in a process
- Present interesting material then move to more serious needs
- Use a random sequencing
- Dependency on linked events or learning
- Change the *knowledge* aspects to *doing* something related to this knowledge gain
- *Doing* (an assessed practical event) to *knowledge* (based on the level determined from the practical event) to DOING (further practical application)

Whichever model you use will depend on a variety of factors, most of which you will need to have obtained in your earlier analysis of the audience - what they know, what level of understanding they have – linked with the nature and complexity of the subject.

Unless it is a very simple subject, whichever model is chosen a *step* approach will be essential with the material broken down into easily digestible steps, stages or parts. The commonly quoted question is 'How do you eat an elephant?' with the answer 'In bite-sized chunks'.

Do the same with your material and the audience will be able to digest it more readily.

Putting a proposition

Presenters can be completely baffled on occasions when their presentations are not as successful as the same one given on other occasions, or a message that is felt to be so very important is simply not accepted by the audience. What has gone wrong? It may simply be that the message is not as important or useful as was thought, and the audience recognizes this, or the current, non-accepting audience is quite different from the others and is from a group or hierarchy that has widely varying views from those of the presenter.

But often rejection is due to the way the proposal has been put forward.

'*Readers – you will do as I tell you because my way is the best.*' How did you react on reading that sentence? Probably your hackles started to rise because what I was doing was not only *telling* you what you had to do, but also saying that I knew best, rather than accomodating any views you might hold. Transfer this approach to the presentation. If people are *told* what to do there is a chance that they will react against this and the presentation is wasted. The alternative approach that has been shown to be more successful in a variety of situations is to *suggest* their consideration of the proposition. 'How do you feel about such and such an approach? My reasons for suggesting this are. . .' or 'I would like you to consider this rather different approach'. Because an appeal is being made to them rather than their being told, this appeal is frequently heard with considerably more receptive feelings.

QUESTIONING TECHNIQUES

Some smaller and less formal presentation groups lend themselves to active participation, and one of the ways in which the presenter can encourage participation and discussion is to pose questions to the audience – the reverse of the situation at the end of the presentation when the audience poses questions to the presenter.

Question formats

A question only deserves a response at the level at which it is posed – ask a silly question and you should expect a silly answer! Although this is not a 100 percent golden rule, certain types of questions are more likely to receive certain types of answers.

Consequently, if you intend to ask questions of the audience at any time during the presentation, these questions should be prepared in advance and included in the brief in the same way as other presentation material.

Questions can be posed in a variety of ways and in many cases the response is based on the format of the question.

- **Closed questions.** These normally require (and obtain) a simple 'yes' or 'no' answer or a straightforward statement of facts, eg 'Have you ever conducted an appraisal interview?' or 'Who was your last employer?' Questions of this nature usually require that another question be asked immediately, unless that is all the information you require.
- **Presumptive questions.** These are usually closed questions that assume part of the answer, eg (without any previous information) 'What sort of car do you drive?' This assumes that the other person has a car and that they can drive.
- **Leading questions.** These tend to be negatively presumptive questions that obviously suggest that the questioner is expecting a certain answer. This may put the other person on the spot, depending on their relationship with the questioner. For example, 'I expect you will want to start your appraisal interview programme without any further training or delay?'
- **Multiple questions.** These are in fact a series of questions strung together. They can cause problems for the responder who may not remember all the parts of the question and consequently (or sometimes deliberately) answer one part only – usually the last part. For example, 'Have you got a driving licence? When did you get it and what groups is it for? Where did you take your test? Can you drive a range of vehicles?'
- **Rambling questions.** Similar to the multiple question but without the specifically identifiable parts of that type of question. The rambling question goes on and on until the listener is unsure what is being asked.
- **Conflict questions.** These are designed to produce a reaction from the other person and may (whether intentionally or not) produce a negative or emotional response. If an emotional response does not emerge, it may be that emotions are being suppressed, eg 'I might have expected you to react like that, mightn't I?'
- **Hypothetical questions.** Usually intended to test a responder's problem-solving ability by posing a hypothetical situation, eg 'If

you were given an unlimited budget to set up a learning resource centre, how would you go about this?' This type of question *can* test ability and knowledge, but being hypothetical may receive only a hypothetical response.

- **Open questions.** Usually begin with *what, how, why* and, less openly, *who, where* and *when*. They are used to open up the discussion as the response is less likely to be monosyllabic, eg 'How would you describe an appraisal interview?' They can also be an invitation to give extended information, eg 'Tell me about some of the experiences you have had in the appraisal interviews you have conducted'.

- **Probing questions.** These are open questions which seek further or clarified information on responses already given, eg 'You said you had done so and so. Can you tell me more about that work?' One of the instant types of question the presenter should be prepared to ask, particularly if the responder(s) to the original question have been vague, evasive or have given incomplete answers.

- **Testing understanding.** A variation on the probing question that sets out to ensure that the questioner has put over a point correctly, the other person has understood what the questioner has asked or said, or the questioner has understood what the responder has said. For example, 'If I've got it right you are suggesting that. . . . Is that right?'

- **Reflection.** This does not appear as a question, but its basic intention is to encourage the responder to give more information without having to be asked a question directly. If the other person has made a brief comment such as 'I'm having some problems with the new procedure', but appears unwilling to extend this information, a reflection might be 'It seems that the problem is mainly with the new procedure'. Hopefully, the other person will then say 'Yes, that's right. What I am being asked to do is. . . .'

HANDLING DIFFICULT REPLIES

If you ask a question of the audience, you are expecting a response and, if you have posed the question in the most effective manner, you will receive a response more or less in the form you anticipated or hoped for. But not all responses will fall into these categories and you must be prepared to deal with them effectively. Often, when planning the session and the questions you will ask, it is possible to identify the occasions when the responses may be other than those desired.

- **When the answer is incorrect or incomplete.** Do not ridicule, be sarcastic or ignore it. Show appreciation for a response and acknowledge any incomplete part that is correct. Then pass to the remainder and either correct it or, better still, probe for the correct answer, initially with the responder and if necessary with the remainder of the group.
- **When the answer is woolly but the responder had the correct answer in mind.** Check that the rest of the audience understands what was said by testing understanding, either straightforwardly or by asking another member to give his or her impression or response.
- **When the question is received with silence.** Ask yourself 'Was the question clear?' Had you overestimated the group's ability? Break the question into smaller steps. The silence may be accompanied by puzzled looks – this will indicate to you non-verbally that they have not understood rather than have some other reason for not responding.
- **When the response asks for your views.** This is a ploy often used by people either to put you on the spot or to avoid having to commit themselves. State openly in response that you know (or don't know) the answer, but you would prefer them to provide the information.
- **When a frequent responder gives a quick, correct answer.** Thank the responder then check that the remainder have heard and understood or accept the response, or whether anyone else can add anything.

HOW DO YOU PRESENT YOURSELF?

Personal techniques

However good or bad, complex or simple, interesting or uninteresting the material, it is up to the presenter to project it to the audience, and the presenter's manner and personal skills can either make or break the presentation.

Using your voice

The four Ps

In Chapter 2 alliteration and the four Ps were introduced as a memory aid. These relate to the way the voice is used in a presentation.

- ■ **P**roject your voice
- ■ **P**ronounce your words carefully
- ■ **P**ause frequently
- ■ **P**ace should be varied

Projection. This is important, particularly when you are not used to speaking in public or not used to speaking in rooms larger than your own. It will be of little use if you have some wonderful material and messages if the people at the rear of the audience cannot hear you. So you will need to throw your voice to the back of the room. Try this out with a colleague sitting at the back of the room as you try speaking with different volumes until the most appropriate one is obvious. However, with a full audience present, there will be coughs, breathing, chairs scraping and creaking, so it will be necessary to raise the volume a step or so from the one you found in the rehearsal.

Pronunciation. Have you a regional accent? Does it matter? Are you on 'home' ground? With a more national audience, would your accent interfere with their understanding? You may have to try to modify a strong regional accent, but do not be ashamed of it. It must, however, be understood by people who are not familiar with it.

Words, particularly their endings, are easily lost in a largish audience – so pronounce your words slightly more than you do in normal conversation. In complex, multi-syllable words, accentuate the syllables so that the whole word is clear. But watch that this does not become artificial.

Are you likely to use any difficult words, particularly any with which you have had problems in the past? Check their pronunciation and rehearse this until it ceases to be a problem, or find a different word to use.

Pause. Do this frequently so that both you and the audience can catch up with what has been said. Pauses can also be used for effect – a pause (say for a silent count of four) before an important word or statement can alert the audience to the fact that something they should listen to is coming. Don't be worried by silences – they will seem longer to you than to your audience.

Pace. This should be varied, not only to break a monotonous delivery but also for effect. If you increase the speed of delivery, this can suggest importance or excitement and the audience can be stimulated to increase their reception speed. Slow the delivery down and the words then become more dramatic and again demonstrate importance. The tone and pitch of your voice should also be varied for interest and impact, and repetition of key words or phrases in a different tone, at a different speed or with different emphases will also draw attention to these points.

As mentioned earlier, you should aim to talk at a rather slower speed than normal, particularly if you are a normally rapid talker. It may sound to you as if you are speaking too slowly, but not to the listeners, who are being given the opportunity of hearing your words rather than having to race their minds to keep up with you. However, don't overdo this, as too slow a pace might suggest a lack of enthusiasm on your part and a resultant drop in their enthusiasm.

MERK

The other major mnemonic used in remembering aspects about the control of the voice in presentations is MERK.

- **M**odulate
- **E**mphasize
- **R**epeat
- **K**eep eyes from notes

Modulate the tone of your voice to keep it interesting – use drama, apparent monotony, harshness, softness and so on.

Emphasize certain parts of the speech for effect.

Repeat key words and phrases to emphasize their importance and ensure understanding and recall.

Keep your eyes away from your notes as much as possible. Otherwise your volume will drop, you may seem to mumble and your credibility will fall if it appears that you are simply reading from a script.

VERBAL MANNERISMS

Whether we are aware of them or not, we all have mannerisms, verbal and non-verbal, that are part of our make-up. Many of these become more apparent when we are under stress, and giving a presentation is certainly classified as a stressful situation. These mannerisms, to a large extent, are part of our unique identity, and under normal circumstances getting rid of them would detract from our personality. But if they are excessive when we are giving a presentation there is a danger that they will get in the way and reduce the effectiveness of our event. Get to know your mannerisms and decide what you have to do about them. Usually there is something you can do: either reduce their frequency or obviousness or eradicate them altogether. Otherwise the audience will soon become distracted and may concentrate on them rather than on the presentation.

UMs and ARRRs

Anyone who has heard or seen themselves delivering a talk on audio cassette or video will have been surprised at the number of times they start a sentence with 'Um' or 'Arrr'. (I was horrified when I first heard myself.) The frequency of these openings increases when speakers are not sure about what they are going to say next or when confidence is low, so to fill in what would be a short silence they throw in an 'Um'. Avoid this, as short silences are much less noticeable than an increasing number of noises, and if they are excessive the audience will notice them and react to them, and someone will start counting the number of times you do it. If you are hesitant about what to say next, say nothing until you are ready to speak, then say words, don't make noises.

Similarly, common 'noises', although appearing to the words, are unconscious expressions, used particularly under stress. 'OK' can be a statement or question, and too much repetition can result in the audience responding 'OK' on each occasion – this is reminiscent of a pantomime reaction rather than a serious presentation. Another common 'noise' made by quite a lot of people is 'You know', used on many occasions, usually unnecessarily. Remember you have a limited time to put over your message; superfluous words and noises reduce this time, with unwanted side effects.

Some people, perhaps originally deliberately, pronounce some words in a way that makes them very obvious. The audience will quickly identify these and may take too much notice of the pronunciation, to the detriment of the words themselves. For example, a colleague always pronounced 'to' as 'tuh' and after a while it became surprising how often he needed to say 'to' – we knew because we started counting! We may choose to use uncommon, alternative pronunciation. I developed a habit of pronouncing 'questionnaire' starting with 'k' rather than 'qwe', but soon realized that this pronunciation annoyed some people. (I didn't always stop saying it my way, but I told people what I was doing, then avoided using the word as much as possible – it would probably have been simpler to use the common pronunciation!)

BREATHING

I don't want to overload you with too many 'dos' and 'don'ts' so that you are thinking more about these than about your presentation, but many of them make the difference between an excellent presentation and one that is less effective. If you identify that you have several aspects to modify, do so slowly, and not all at once. Efficient breathing can help you considerably during a presentation, particularly, as already mentioned, at the start of the event. It was suggested that before going 'on stage' you took a number of slow, deep breaths, breathing in down to your stomach so that your diaphragm is lowered and your heart rate starts to be controlled. It is also good practice to do this during the presentation when there is a natural or deliberate pause – Murphy's butterflies are always ready to swoop again if they are given the opportunity!

The concept behind this controlled breathing is that the brain requires an ample supply of oxygen to enable it to function efficiently. The lungs, if supplied with a plentiful supply of air in a regular manner, will perform this oxygenation successfully.

In the stress of an event you may forget to breathe correctly, in which case some breathing training is recommended. There are a number of different methods available, each suggesting various exercises, but if you do not need to, or do not want to go this far, deep, regular breathing will produce some improvement. If you are sitting to give your presentation, how you sit is doubly important, because if you are sitting slouched in a chair, your body folded and crumpled, your breathing will not be nearly as effective as if you were sitting upright, using the muscles in your body, including those controlling your breathing. Sit up, shoulders back, chest out!

SOME FINAL THOUGHTS ON MAKING YOUR POINTS

During your presentation you should:

- Consider whether to stand or sit, and where
- Keep the 'looking' techniques in mind
- Make your main points in a structured and sequenced way
- Suggest rather than tell
- Use your voice effectively
- Breathe correctly

Some further, final suggestions for effective presenting include the following.

- Keep to a minimum
- Signal your intentions
- Use examples and analogies
- Use plenty of graphics
- Respond to the audience's needs
- Answer their unspoken 'What's in it for me?'
- Summarize

Keep to a minimum

There is always the temptation to try to tell them everything. Rarely will you have time to do this and, even if you had, by the end of the period the minds of your audience would be on the beach of a Pacific island, mending the car, having a beauty treatment or whatever. Stick to a small number of key features; rely on questions at the end to introduce other aspects about which the audience has an obvious interest; provide a comprehensive handout to satisfy the needs of those who want to know more. This should be possible if you stick to a 15-minute (maximum) talk (with graphics etc) and leave at least that time for a question and answer period.

Signal your intentions

Let the audience know what is coming next (and perhaps wake them up) by signalling what your next topic is going to be. You can use such signals as:

'What I'd like to do now is. . .'
'What I'd like to talk about/help us look at now is. . .'
'Let's summarize what we have looked at to this point'.

Be careful, however, not to overuse this technique as it can become annoying.

Other signals are made by using recognizably distinctive words:

'Significant'
'Important'
'Key to the matter', and so on.

Use examples and analogies

Real life examples and analogies with situations with which the audience are familiar will help them to relate what you are saying to their own experience. Difficult and complex issues, terms or procedures can often be simplified by using an analogy, preferably one with which the audience is familiar.

Use plenty of graphics

The use of aids has been dealt with earlier, but the value of pictures, drawings, photographs, or word slides cannot be overstressed. In addition to bringing your words to life, these aids break up the talking time and extend the audience attention span. But again, don't overdo it and make your presentation an all-singing, all-dancing picture show – words used correctly can have a significant impact.

Respond to the audience needs and answer their unspoken 'What's in it for me?'

Audiences commonly attend a presentation to get something out of it for themselves – information, learning, direction, the chance to comment etc. Try to determine their objectives in addition to ensuring that yours are satisfied, and give them the opportunity, whether as part of your approach or in a question and discussion period, to satisfy theirs.

Summarize

Do not assume that your audience is hanging on your every word and remembering everything you say, however much they may wish to do so. Help them to remember, and at the same time introduce one of the 'attention span triggers' by stopping at a convenient point and summarizing what has been said so far – repetition is one of the main tools in aiding retention and recall. Make this summary short and impactive and don't fall into the trap of repeating virtually every thing you have said, so defeating the object of the 'summary'.

USING LANGUAGE

Our language is a rich and powerful one, and you should use it to the maximum to enhance your presentation. Here are some tips on how to do this.

- Choose your words carefully
- Use 'power' words
- Avoid jargon
- Create phrases to remember
- Avoid long sentences
- Use exciting and active verbs
- Avoid foreign words and Latin tags
- Avoid abbreviations

Choose your words carefully

Many similar words have completely different meanings – ensure you are using the appropriate one. A number of words mean the same thing – which one would be the most appropriate for your audience and can you use the others to avoid over repetition? Do not become a slave to language rules, otherwise you may seem pedantic, however altruistic your motives for the *mot juste*.

Use 'power' words

These direct the audience's attention to what you are saying, wake them up, and can act as breaks in their falling attention span. If you use colourless language your message will be colourless, lacking impact and interest. Use such words as 'interesting, urgent, unusual, powerful, significant, substantial, exciting, new, critical, compelling' which are attention getting without being flowery or too obvious. However, do not over-use these words as repetition will reduce their impact. If they are included in a sentence intended to grab attention, eg 'This is a really important matter to which we must address ourselves in an urgent way', most people will mentally prepare themselves for the key statement of the presentation. But, of course, you must not follow such a signalling device with a whimper.

Avoid jargon

The general advice to presenters is to avoid jargon as is can be incomprehensible, misunderstood, and often simply annoy the audience. However, there are situations when it can help you.

If you are speaking to an audience that you *know beyond any doubt* will understand all the jargon you might use, use it, otherwise you may have to over-simplify a description and the audience might feel you are being patronizing. Using jargon with which they are familiar shows that you are on their side and want the occasion to be interactive.

Even if you are not part of the culture of an audience that has common roots and knowledge, use some of their jargon. This lets them know that you have taken the trouble to find out about the language they speak and the environment in which they work. But be sure you are using the jargon in the correct way and don't overdo it, because if you are not fully at home with it you are almost certain to slip up.

If it's your jargon you want to use, don't – if the audience does not understand it readily, they will simply stop listening. If you must use it, then equally you must explain what it means, and if you have to explain it, why use it?

Create phrases to remember

Very few people who experienced the 1939–45 war in Britain will have forgotten Churchill's famous catchphrase: 'We shall fight on the beaches, we shall fight on the landing grounds, we shall fight in the fields and in the streets, we shall fight in the hills; we shall never surrender'. Few of us have the skill of creating memorable phrases such as this, but a little thought can often produce something that will catch the audience's interest. How many people's lives have been saved by their remembering, probably unconsciously, the oft-quoted catch-phrase of several years ago, 'Klunk, click, every trip'.

Avoid long sentences

Long written sentences are frequently difficult to read and understand; this applies equally with the spoken word. By the time you have reached the end of a long and complicated sentence, the listeners have forgotten why you started. Keep your sentences *quite* short – 'quite' short because if they are too short they may be equally difficult to understand, and a series of these sounds more like staccato barking than an interactive 'conversation'.

Use exciting and active verbs

Verbs are the doing parts of a sentence, the parts where the action is or should be. Make them exciting (see 'power' words earlier) and, though you may be striving for simplicity, consider whether a different verb might create an even more dramatic picture. You may be 'asking' for something: can you use begging, pleading, imploring, demanding, directing oneself to, taking information about, making a searching enquiry, investigating, conducting a census, canvass, survey, market research, poll, public opinion poll, straw poll or vote, vote probe, test, means test, check, spot check or trial run? A thesaurus is as invaluable when preparing the words in your presentation as a dictionary.

Avoid foreign words and Latin tags

Do not use foreign words unless they are ones that are fully integrated in our language. Similarly, Latin tags may endear you to academic scholars, but to the majority of people in audiences they are unknowns and give the idea that you are trying to impress with your knowledge and learning. By all means use them if the culture and environment is right, otherwise use plain language. I have recounted how I am guilty of pronouncing 'questionnaire' in a different way. Look earlier in this section under 'choosing words' when I employed *mot juste* – this is a simple French phrase, but some of your audience might react with 'What's that!' It is as easy to say 'the right word'.

Avoid abbreviations

Beware the use of abbreviations, in the same way as jargon. You may know the meaning of the abbreviation, but are you sure that your audience does, or has the same interest in talking shorthand? Use the guidelines described under 'jargon'.

ENDING YOUR PRESENTATION EFFECTIVELY

Ending a presentation is often as difficult as starting. The simplest advice comes from the colloquialism 'Put up and shut up' or, once you have said what you have to say, stop talking. However, ending a presentation effectively is not as simple as this. The objectives that you have for the end of the event are that the audience:

- has understood the presentation and learned from it;
- remembers what you have said, particularly the significant key points;
- recalls these points after the event and takes the required action.

There can be more specific objectives, too.

- Remind them of the content of the presentation and in particular the key points
- Ask them to do something after the event – a general exhortation is not sufficient; make specific recommendations about what they can do
- Have them think about what you have talked about – ask a question for them to take away with them
- Leave them with choices – a limited number of specific choices for positive action
- Instil fear of or concern about not taking the action described in your presentation, not as a threat but as a warning of the consequences.

In order to try to achieve these objectives there are two specific actions you can take before you close. You might have allowed a period for questions or discussion at the end of the event – manage this before ending the presentation. One common failing of presenters is to 'end' the presentation only to have it start up again with the questions or discussion – these are part of the presentation and should have been planned and prepared for.

The first specific ending action is to 'tell 'em what you have told 'em' – in other words summarize the key points of your presentation, particularly any specific proposals. Be as brief as you can while being comprehensive, but do not in effect repeat your presentation. State the key points and in a sentence or two summarize their content and any required action.

Then end as you started, with impact, so that the audience goes away with your message firmly and positively in their minds. The summary, if presented in a different or dramatic way, can serve this purpose. If you started with an impact slide, the same slide can be presented to show that what you intended to do has been achieved (make certain that it has!).

The use of an Expectations Chart at the start of the presentation was discussed in Chapter 8, it was suggested that the summarized flipchart might be displayed. Reference back to it can be useful at the end of the presentation, when the satisfaction of hopes and expectations might be discussed and the position clarified about members' worries or concerns – were these justified; do any still exist; what can be done to clear them up? Remember, however, that resolving any residuals might take additional time or other approaches agreed. A fully satisfied Expectations Chart will take only a few minutes to clear, but do not anticipate that this will be the situation every time.

At all costs make the ending positive; do not just let the presentation tail away to nothing. There is considerable evidence that, even if the audience remembers little of the main topics you have presented, if the ending is strong they will go away remembering this, at least. Here are some useful closing approaches (sometimes pilloried as clichés):

'So in conclusion I should like to say...'
'Just before I close, can I say...'
'And finally, before I open this up for questions...'
'I should like you to go away with this thought...'

But certainly not:

'Well that's all I have to say, so I'll stop here'. (This is hardly likely to put the audience in a frame of mind to ask questions.)

AN ENDING CHECKLIST

To confirm that you are ending your presentation as effectively and completely as you can, ask yourself the following questions.

- Did I put over effectively the key points?
- Was the main part of the presentation given effectively?
- Did I stimulate questions from the audience?
- Is the audience likely to be going away still considering the presentation material?
- Did the verbal and/or non-verbal signals from the audience show that they had appreciated the presentation?
- Did I ensure that the audience knew they could ask questions?
- Did I answer all the questions satisfactorily?
- Did I admit that I didn't know an answer and promise to take some action?
- Did I summarize the presentation effectively and comprehensively?
- Did I end the presentation in a calm and unhurried manner?
- Was the audience clear that the presentation was complete?

SOME ACTIVITIES TO CONSIDER

ACTIVITY

Either,

1. Give each person a copy of a book and ask them to read aloud a selected passage as if they were presenting this to an audience. The reading can be recorded on an audio recorder or with video for playback and self-assessment.

Or,

2. A book passage can be issued as in 1, but in this case the passage would be 'presented' to the remainder of the group for eventual feedback.

10

Handling Questions and Questioners; Obtaining Evaluation Feedback

This chapter:

- suggests techniques for handling questions from the audience, including difficult questions and difficult audience members
- provides a means of self-assessing your performance and obtaining feedback from others.

AN END-OF-PRESENTATION QUESTIONING STRATEGY

Where questions are invited at the end of the presentation, you must know exactly how you are going to handle them. Up to this stage you have been in almost complete control, unless you have allowed ongoing interruptions, but by inviting questions you are passing a major part of that control to the audience. Not only are they able to ask almost anything they wish, but you may find some difficulty in constraining individuals to asking questions or making brief statements – a major problem is when a member of the audience starts to give their own presentation instead of asking a question!

The role of questions in a presentation can have a number of objectives, from both the presenter's and the audience's points of view.

As far as the presenter is concerned, questions posed can be used to:

- assess how effective the presentation has been
- determine the extent of the interest you have generated
- identify any areas which are unclear
- change the presentation atmosphere from a passive to an active one
- change the presentation from a lecture to an interactive event
- provide further information and views more deeply than those expressed in the main body of the presentation
- satisfy any specific needs of the audience

When the audience ask questions, they:

- seek clarification of areas they did not understand
- seek extension of the information given
- want to gain more information about the views, opinions and feelings of the presenter
- want to check out the credibility of the presenter's expertise
- use questions as a means of expressing their own views

At the start of your presentation you should have advised the audience of the questioning policy: that there will be no questions, that questions may be posed at any time, or that questions should be held until the end of the presentation when time will be allocated.

Not to allow questions at all, unless you are making other arrangements for subsequent clarification and extension, is a very dangerous practice because, however superb a presenter you feel you are, there will always be people with doubts or who did not understand you. Your objectives have failed if you do not make provision for satisfying their needs. The problem can be solved to some extent by issuing a clear handout after the presentation, but the most effective approach is to announce that you, or someone, will be available to answer questions and deal with problems.

The most natural way of dealing with questions is to accept them as you are proceeding with the presentation. This immediately solves the problem in the listener's mind and it also shows you that you may not have explained some aspect as well as you could have done, or thought you did. But this approach can cause havoc with your timing, because once you have accepted one question there will almost certainly be others.

The more common approach is to accept questions at the end. You will have allocated a period of time for this when timing your presentation, which you can then control. Unfortunately some questions that should be asked are never asked, usually because the listener has by that time forgotten the question, or is so frustrated by having to wait that they no longer want to ask the question. On the other side of the coin, the question that might have disturbed your flow might well have been answered a little later in the talk.

On balance, the most frequent decision is to leave the question period to the end, in which case you must do four things.

---

1. You must ensure that you leave sufficient time at the end, otherwise the audience will leave in a frustrated mood and this will interfere with the acceptance and recall of your message.
2. You must describe your questioning strategy at the start of the presentation.
3. Listen carefully when a question is asked. Avoid the danger of assuming what the question is about when the questioner is half-way through. Often the crunch, or real question, comes at the end.
4. You must deal with every question in some way, however difficult it may be. Remember, you invited the audience to pose questions.

Opening the presentation to questions at the relevant time requires careful handling. If we assume that you have created rapport with the audience and have made an effective presentation, questions will usually follow your invitation. *But do not assume that this will happen.*

Following the completion of the presentation section of your event, two feelings may be uppermost in your mind when you invite questions.

1. Nobody will ask a question and I shall look and feel a fool just standing here.
2. I won't be able to answer the first question and again will look and feel a fool.

You cannot force the audience to ask questions, but there are techniques you can employ to make it easier for both them and you. You can be fairly certain that there will be people with questions they want to raise or comments they want to make, but this may not happen as nobody wants to be the first to speak. You may have to help these people and others who are hesitant about making themselves 'visible'.

The usual way of introducing the question period is simply to remind the audience what you had stated earlier, and invite them to ask any questions or seek clarification. The result will be either the start of an effective questioning period or a deathly silence, the latter being commonly faced by presenters. If questioning commences, answer fully, openly, honestly and to the best of your ability, admitting your ignorance if you cannot answer, but, as suggested earlier, offering to get back to the questioner.

If there is silence, do not give the impression that this is throwing you. Wait a short period for a delayed question to appear, then comment in as natural a way as possible that:

'I am often asked at this stage in this presentation, what...'

and 'answer' this question. Have such a question ready in your presentation planning.

In the majority of cases, this breaks the ice and questions from the audience follow. However, if no questions emerge, prolonging the agony does not help post-presentation acceptance, so it may be relevant then to say:

'There seem to be no questions, so let us close now'.

If this seems too unhelpful or abrupt a close, modify it by adding that you will be available for individual questions after the close, or suggest that any lingering questions might be satisfied by the full handout that is available.

An alternative to taking what may be seen as draconian action by just closing the event if the audience doesn't respond is to use the buzz group approach.

BUZZ GROUPS

Although one of the reasons for a non-responsive audience may be the way in which you have posed the question, there are others. The audience may simply be a very quiet group, unwilling to express themselves openly. If this appears to be the case, or if you want the group as a whole to consider a question you have posed, use the buzz group approach. This is a reduced form of that used in training and, of course, this approach can be used. But in closing many presentations it is not always appropriate to separate the audience in this way.

The buzz group here requires the audience to turn their chairs so that they form small groups of three or four. Each group then considers for a short period of time:

- what questions they wish to ask you;
- what responses they want to give to questions posed by you.

The 'buzz' results from the talk emanating from a number of small groups in the same room. Following the discussions in the buzz groups, the questions or views are then expressed to the full group. One major advantage, apart from introducing activity into the presentation, is that questions or views can emerge anonymously. The buzz group can elect a representative who will express the views of the group.

This approach will almost certainly produce more questions or views than other methods and you should be prepared for this, both in terms of responding and the availability of sufficient time.

HANDLING DIFFICULT QUESTIONS

Not every question that might be posed will be ones that you can answer simply and easily. Complex answers require your skill in making them clear and easily understood. But other types of difficult questions can be posed by members of the audience. These include:

- the question that isn't a question
- the incomplete question
- the irrelevant question
- the long and/or multiple question
- the 'trap'
- 'Monopoly'
- the question to which you do not know the answer
- your mind goes blank when the question is posed

The question that isn't a question

Usually the questioner takes a long time to pose this 'question' and when they finish you realize that there wasn't a question after all. You have two options: either thank the individual for their contribution and continue by asking a question or seeking other views; or thank the individual and use the 'politician's twist' – say 'I think the question you are asking is...' and give a response to the question that you feel should have been asked.

The incomplete question

Some questions may be too short to be generally understood, although you are aware of the questioner's intention. A useful approach is to rephrase the question by suggesting that, if you have heard it correctly, the questioner is asking about so-and-so. Suggest that other people may be interested in this aspect and widen your answer to the extent that you feel the questioner intended or that is useful in presenting your views. This approach is also useful if the questioner is near the front and has asked the question in a voice so quiet that you know the rest of the audience will not have heard it.

The irrelevant question

This can often be simply a means for the individual to state their own views, which may have little to do with the subject being discussed. It may indeed be a question, but irrelevant. Again, thank the speaker for their 'interesting point or point-of-view', but as time is limited you must keep the discussion strictly to the subject.

Sometimes the irrelevancy is due to the listener having missed the point of the presentation, or part of it. This can place you in a quandary as this questioner may be expressing the views of the remainder of the audience – you obviously failed to make that point clear. In this case you must quickly recap the point and ensure that it is clear and understood on this occasion. Or, if there is a handout, refer the audience to the specific part of the handout that explains the point. If, however, it is evident that the questioner is the only one who has missed the point, your response can be that to repeat the information would take up too much of the limited time. Either offer to discuss it with them afterwards, or again, if relevant, refer them to the handout.

The long and/or multiple question

The two principal options in this case are either your acceptance of the question or putting the onus back on the questioner. If you take the first approach, as the questioner is reeling off a number of questions within the one contribution, you can be noting each to answer when the list is complete. Otherwise, ask the questioner to re-pose the most important part of the question. In theory the latter approach should save time and make your response easier, but there is always the danger that you will be faced with the full list again!

The trap

You have to be able to recognize the trap in questions – and avoid it as far as possible or respond effectively. This should not be too difficult if you know your subject well. If you have made the same presentation on a number of occasions you will probably have experienced this type of question, so you can be prepared for it. Falling into the trap, however, this becomes part of *your* learning process! If there appear to be very negative reasons why the trap has been set, ask the questioner why they asked this question or type of question – ie, what their hidden agenda may be.

'Monopoly'

There is always the danger that the more active members or those with the loudest voices might try to monopolize the question period, often using this to over-air their own views rather than seek information or clarification. You must identify this at an early stage and take steps to change the situation, without antagonizing the monopolizers or anyone else. A useful approach is to acknowledge the contribution and move on. You can say, for example, without being patronizing, 'Now that was a very good point. But time is speeding past, so what other questions from others in the audience are there?'

The question to which you do not know the answer

Comments on this have been made previously but you should also consider 'Shame on you!'. If it happens you must immediately admit your lack of knowledge and offer to obtain the information and get back to them as quickly as possible – and do it.

An alternative might be to ask if any member of the audience knows the answer and would like to contribute. But even a knowledgeable member may not be prepared to come forward, so you will have to offer to answer later. *If this happens too often, however, you have obviously not prepared sufficiently.*

Your mind goes blank when the question is posed

You know you should know the answer, but your mind goes blank. Do not panic – this could make things worse. Give yourself a few moments to collect your thoughts – the pause will seem longer to you than to the audience. One overused technique to gain time is to respond immediately with, 'That is an interesting question. Let me think about this to ensure I give you the best answer'. This has been used so often that many audiences will know what you are doing. Another ploy that is often seen as avoidance – even though it may not be – is to ask whether anyone would like to make any comments on the question posed.

An acceptable alternative that can endear you to the audience – provided you do not have to do it too frequently – is to admit what has happened and ask for a few moments to get your act together.

DIFFICULT GROUPS AND PEOPLE

Difficult people and situations usually surface at the end of the main body of a presentation, when the floor is opened to questions. There are many possible ways of dealing with difficulties during your presentation caused by your audience, whether this is small or large. The techniques will work with some presenters and with some people, but the same approach will not necessarily work in the same way in two apparently similar situations. The reason for this is that, usually, people are 'difficult' (albeit in the same way) for different reasons, and in many cases these reasons are not obvious and may never emerge; for example, the person may have taken a dislike to you from the start; they may have been sent unwillingly to the event; some personal burden is weighing them down and making them behave in a manner unusual for them. All you have to go on is the observed behaviour and you must try various ways of dealing effectively with this. You cannot hope to change the internal motivation of the person, but you may be able to get them to modify their behaviour.

Whatever the problems you must do *something*, otherwise the disturbing effect caused by the individual(s) will either be transmitted to the remainder of the audience, or the remainder will fail to get from the presentation everything that they want.

Although there are many potential difficulties, embryonic presenters should not go in fear and trembling of these situations. In my experience major difficulties are rare since, even though all members of the audience may not be with you, the ones against frequently do nothing overtly. They simply take little notice of what you do and say. Problems are more frequently caused after the presentation in the audience's informal discussions, to which you are rarely a party. Often the only indication you have of this is when you overhear a comment such as 'Well I for one am not going to take any notice of all that!' or

'Wasn't that just a waste of time'. However, if you do overhear such comments, you should do all you can to determine the extent of the feeling, because if it is widespread you have failed in your objectives.

HANDLING DIFFICULT PEOPLE

There are potentially many people who can cause you problems during or at the end of your presentation, usually when you invite questions and discussion. There are guidelines for dealing with some of these, but remember that your skill may not be sufficient to handle them or they may simply refuse to be handled. In the latter case you may have to be firm and positive, and politely tell them that, for example, this is not the time and/or place to discuss this matter; there is insufficient time to do justice to it, so another occasion would be more appropriate; the subject is not one that is of interest to the audience, or the comment does not fall within the presentation's range so you are unable to discuss it. These may seem hard, but remember that the difficult person is only one individual, and you have to consider the vast majority of the audience (who are probably supporting you in any case!).

Many difficulties can be avoided by anticipating arguments that may arise from areas of potential conflict that are included in your presentation. Either deal with the areas in a balanced way during the presentation or defuse a question by introducing the subject yourself at the start of the question session – 'I know some people will be thinking...'; 'Well, I should like to say...'. You may still get disagreement, but it will probably be less emotive.

You may encounter any of these types in both large and small audiences. There follow some guidelines on how to deal with them effectively.

- The heckler
- The know-it-all
- The complainer
- The hostile member
- The early bird
- The interrupter
- The dominator
- The irrelevant questioner

The heckler

Hecklers are seldom found in serious, worthwhile presentations. They are more likely to be present at political, union or shareholders' meetings and try to make their presence felt by calling out, usually with irrelevant comments, while someone is speaking. They are frequently unsettled people for whom this is perhaps their only way of being noticed, or they get their 'kicks' from annoying others. They cannot be ignored, as this does not deter them and you may not have a strong-arm brigade to eject them!

Dealing with them

- Never be upset by them or lose your temper
- Perhaps thank them for their comment and move on
- Perhaps find something of merit in what they say, briefly recognize this and move on
- Rephrase the comment into a sensible question and respond to this
- Comment carefully that what they are saying is not relevant to the presentation and they are impeding other members of the audience from listening
- Offer to discuss the subject with them after the presentation

The know-it-all

This is someone who, whenever they are given the opportunity (and sometimes without waiting for this) must say something – usually in the form of their opinion rather than information or a question. They are frequently longwinded and appear simply to be showing off or they are in fact informed, and intent on showing this to everybody.

Dealing with them

- Wait for an opportunity, for example when they pause to take breath or otherwise give you an opening, and thank them for their contribution. Then pass on to either someone else's question or a comment from you
- At first the opportunity break in and thank them. Ask the rest of the audience, either:
  - does anybody want to add anything to what has just been said? or
  - is this subject worth spending any further time on? (Hopefully you will get definite 'Nos')

The complainer

This member of the audience is very similar to the heckler in that they use the situation to make themselves heard – probably the only occasion when this happens! They may be harbouring a grudge against the subject, an organization or situation, and try to make your presentation a platform to air their grievances. Frequently their interruption is vague or incomplete, and not even connected with the presentation subject.

Dealing with them

- If you feel there may be something positive behind their comment but it has been vague, ask them to be more specific
- If the comment is not relevant to the presentation, thank them and say so, and suggest their complaint should be raised elsewhere
- If they try to continue, repeat the irrelevancy comment and direct a question to the rest of the audience or, turning from the complainer, ask for relevant questions

The hostile member

This person is similar to the complainer and their comments are often complaints, but the question is posed or the statement made in a manner obviously hostile or aggressive towards you. In most cases the hostility is not personal; you are simply the person representing the body about which the complaint is made, or you just happen to be there.

Dealing with them

- Do not be aggressive or hostile in return: this could escalate the situation.
- Try to depersonalize the hostility – 'I know you haven't a personal grudge towards me, so what you seem to be concerned about is…'
- Understand the aggression – 'I know how you must feel, but let's look at it this way…'
- Look for common ground – both of you may care about this same issue; say so and suggest action.
- Settle for the disagreement and move on (but be prepared for a further attack).

The early bird

This is frequently one of the very keen members of the audience so you do not want to put them off or annoy them. However, they may simply be attention seekers. Both types can be dealt with in the same way. They demonstrate their attitudes by interrupting you with a question or comment at an inappropriate time – for example, during your presentation when you have specifically asked for questions to be held until the end.

Dealing with them

■ As with most interrupters, thank them for their interest, but point out that you have particularly asked for contributions/questions to be left to the end, so would they keep a note of their question until then
■ Tell them that you are going to deal with that very point later (this is often true), and you have noted their interest

The interrupter

The 'interrupter' differs from the 'early bird' in that their interruption has aggressive tones.

Dealing with them

■ Remain calm, do not over-react, and remember the vast majority of the audience. If the interrupter appears to be a lone individual, with little or no hostility, deal with them as suggested for the early bird
■ If a lone individual, but the interruptions are aggressive, try the approaches suggested for the hostile member
■ If it seems that they represent a bloc of the audience – 'A number of us want to know...' – comment on the objectives and method of your presentation and continue as planned, asking the interrupter to wait until the end
■ It may be necessary to appeal to the audience to get their views on whether they want to proceed as you suggest or otherwise

The dominator

This person tries to dominate the questioning period to the extent that others are unable to or are dissuaded from asking their questions.

Dealing with them

- Thank them for their obvious interest, saying that as time is limited you would like as many people as possible to have a chance of asking questions
- Invite the rest of the audience to answer or comment on the question – this tends to persuade the dominator to become quiet, but be prepared to follow the first approach

The irrelevant questioner

This is someone who asks questions that are not directly related to the presentation issue, and in which the rest of the audience do not appear to be interested.

Dealing with them

- Thank them for their interest, adding that as the question does not relate to the presentation, you would be pleased to take it up with them after the event
- If it is a topic in which the rest of the audience might be interested, ask openly whether they want you to deal with it. If you receive an obvious positive response, answer the question. If there is a negative response or no overt response, use the approach suggested above

The principal criteria in dealing with all difficult members in an audience are that you must not just ignore them. Thank them for their interest, and follow the suggested relevant action described above. It may be that in some very isolated cases you have to be abrupt and refuse to accept their contribution – if it comes to this, do it.

HOW SUCCESSFUL WAS I?

Feedback on your performance as a presenter is essential if you are to maintain your present skills or, even better, improve them. Without feedback how can you have any objective view of the range of skills that make a presentation effective for the audience? Obtaining this feedback is difficult: you can rarely ask an audience how you performed. Remember, however, that you will have more presentations to give and one of the best ways of improving is to discover what went right and what went wrong at the previous one, then doing something about these. If you tried something you had never attempted previously and it worked, why did it work? Keep a note of this success for future reference when circumstances are appropriate. Or if you tried this approach and it didn't work, why didn't it work? Was it the wrong approach for that situation, or did you simply not perform it well enough? Whatever the reason, you can learn from reviewing the process and applying the learning to future presentations.

Certain environments make this possible – presentations linked with some form of training session, when a direct part of the training is feedback, are valuable occasions, and many presenters attend training events to obtain new skills and practise existing ones. At these events they receive feedback, but afterwards there is rarely the opportunity for effective feedback.

Important presentations will benefit from a live rehearsal with an audience of colleagues or others drawn together for the purpose. Feedback can then be sought in a number of ways, and this practice is highly recommended.

FEEDBACK BY SELF-ASSESSMENT

In many cases feedback will be restricted to your own assessment of your performance, although this must necessarily be highly subjective. Complete self-honesty is demanded, although even this does not ensure effective feedback because you cannot be certain that you are aware of everything you are doing.

Subjective self-questioning

One approach to self-review is to ask yourself a number of questions and try to answer them as honestly and as fully as possible. This review should apply to all aspects of your presentation. Figure 10.1 suggests some of the questions you can ask. A member of the audience can help you with some, particularly colleagues who will give you honest feedback and whose views you value. The ones in italics could certainly be used in this way.

1. *Was the content and depth of your presentational material appropriate for this audience?* If not, what should be changed?
2. Did anything go wrong as far as the environment was concerned – for example seating or other arrangements described earlier?
3. Did any of the equipment fail? Could this failure have been avoided?
4. *Were your presentation aids sufficiently effective for the event? Were they up to date, clean, acceptable?*
5. Were your presentation aids in the most appropriate format for the presentation?
6. Was your brief in the most appropriate format? Were you able to use it easily when necessary? If not, why not and what can you do about it?
7. Did you contain the presentation within the prescribed time? If not, what factors caused you to exceed the time? What could you have done to avoid this?
8. Did you give an opportunity for questions to be asked? When – during the presentation or at the end? Was this the most appropriate strategy?
9. To what extent did this affect your timing of the event?
10. Were you able to answer the questions posed?
11. Were you in control of the event all the time, particularly in any discussion?
12. To what extent did you have butterflies? Were you able to control them? If so, how did you do this?
13. *Did you feel your personal presentational skills were sufficient for the event? If not, in what way? Is there anything you can do about this in the future?*
14. Were you able to read any non-verbal signals being given by the audience? Were you able to react to these in any way?
15. *Were you aware of the non-verbal signals you were giving? Were they congruent with your words?*
16. *Were you aware of your mannerisms? Do you think that the audience noticed them? Do you think they had any effect on the way you were received?*
17. Did you 'lighthouse' your regard of the audience? How did you feel about doing this? *How aware were the audience of your attempts to include them all?*
18. *How aware were you of the extent to which the audience understood your presentation?* How were you aware of this?
19. *How aware were you of the extent to which the audience enjoyed your presentation?* How were you aware of this?
20. *How much of the content of your presentation do you think your audience will be able to recall? How are you aware of this?*
21. *How appropriate was your overall approach to this presentation and this audience? If inappropriate, which approach would have been better? How could you do this?*
22. If you had to give this presentation again, to the same audience, as if for the first time, what changes would you make?

Figure 10.1 *A set of self-assessment questions*

A checklist of core skills

A checklist of core skills can be useful in trying to increase your objectivity in self-assessment. Although the checklist shown in Figure 10.2 is based on a scoring pattern, as with all evaluation questionnaires do not confine your responses to scoring only; leave spaces after the scoring for as much comment as possible, positive as well as negative. Add any other items to the checklist you feel are relevant to your presentation approach.

If you have the opportunity to invite others to appraise your presentation, you will find the checklist in Figure 10.2 useful for a consistent approach or alternatively, you can adapt the questions.

Training workshops in presentational skills are ideal situations in which to obtain both wide-ranging and expert feedback. These workshops include opportunities to practise presenting, followed by feedback to the presenter by the trainer or facilitator and the fellow-learners who have acted as the audience. This feedback can take a variety of forms: simple verbal feedback following the presentation; verbal feedback preceded by a reflective period during which Figures 10.1 and/or 10.2 are completed by the presenter, the audience and the trainer; video recordings perhaps supplemented by verbal feedback; or simply stand-alone self-assessment.

File your completed checklists in the Presentations Log suggested in the Introduction, repeat the process until you are satisfied with your performance, and at intervals thereafter repeat the process as a maintenance activity.

VIDEO FEEDBACK

A valuable replacement of or supplement to the written checklist is the video. Rehearsal and real presentations can be videod and viewed after the event, again using the checklist as a guide. Useful aspects of using video recordings include stopping the video and repeating a particularly interesting section, and being able to play it as many times as necessary. The video can also be copied and sent to others for review at their convenience and eventual feedback.

Presentation Competences	Skill Scale				
	Very effective			Less effective	
Techniques					
Introduction of self	5	4	3	2	I
Introduction of presentation	5	4	3	2	I
Starting attitude:					
enthusiasm	5	4	3	2	I
helpfulness	5	4	3	2	I
non-patronizing	5	4	3	2	I
informative of process	5	4	3	2	I
Use of icebreaker or other activity	5	4	3	2	I
Mapping the presentation process	5	4	3	2	I
Pre-presentation summary	5	4	3	2	I
Interim summaries	5	4	3	2	I
Closing summary	5	4	3	2	I
Discussion leading skill	5	4	3	2	I
Question/answer skill	5	4	3	2	I
Answering questions	5	4	3	2	I
Presentation skills					
Use of Tell, Show, Do where appropriate	5	4	3	2	I
Knowledge of material	5	4	3	2	I
Ability to explain material	5	4	3	2	I
Emphasis of key points	5	4	3	2	I
Flexible approach	5	4	3	2	I
Clear, comprehensive summaries	5	4	3	2	I
Encourages participation/discussion	5	4	3	2	I
Encourages ongoing clarification requests	5	4	3	2	I
Handles interruptions	5	4	3	2	I
Checks for understanding	5	4	3	2	I
Presentation flow	5	4	3	2	I

Figure 10.2 *A self-assessment checklist*

Presentation Competences	Skill Scale				
	Very effective				Less effective

Verbal skills (One of the most subjective self-assessment areas)

Articulate	5	4	3	2	1
Easily understood language	5	4	3	2	1
Avoidance of jargon	5	4	3	2	1
Pleasant manner	5	4	3	2	1
Natural attitude	5	4	3	2	1
Enthusiastic	5	4	3	2	1
Clear	5	4	3	2	1
Easily heard in all parts	5	4	3	2	1
Avoidance of hesitancy	5	4	3	2	1

Personal aspects (The most difficult aspect for self-assessment)

Presenting an acceptable attitude and mien	5	4	3	2	1
Having a pleasing manner	5	4	3	2	1
An acceptable appearance for the situation	5	4	3	2	1
Effective dress	5	4	3	2	1
Effective stance	5	4	3	2	1

Non-verbal skills

Constrained hand gestures	5	4	3	2	1
Non-obtrusive mannerisms	5	4	3	2	1
Effective facial gestures	5	4	3	2	1
Eye contact	5	4	3	2	1
Limited non-verbal noises (ums, ers)	5	4	3	2	1
Congruence of verbal and non-verbal messages	5	4	3	2	1

Presentation aids

Clear visual aids	5	4	3	2	1
Understandable visual aids	5	4	3	2	1
Visual aids visible to all	5	4	3	2	1
Effective use of:					
flipchart	5	4	3	2	1
OHP	5	4	3	2	1
OHP slides	5	4	3	2	1
slides	5	4	3	2	1
video	5	4	3	2	1
computer	5	4	3	2	1
(other aids)	5	4	3	2	1

SOME ACTIVITIES TO CONSIDER

ACTIVITY   Consider a difficult group in which you have been either the presenter or a participant and identify:

1.   Why it was in considered difficult.
2.   How the difficulties – people or processes – were dealt with.
3.   Wheter these processes were effective.
4.   If not, what (else) might have been done to resolve the problems.

ACTIVITY   Discuss with your group some difficult participants you have encountered. Bear in mind the following questions.

1.   In what ways were they difficult?
2.   How were they dealt with (if at all)?
3.   Were these approaches effective?
4.   If not, what action might have been taken to make them more effective?

ACTIVITY   Divide the group into smaller groups and suggest that it would be valuable to each member if they gave each other feedback on some of their observable personal and verbal qualities. Each member should be involved in giving feedback and each member should receive feedback. Possible methods of modifying less effective qualities can then be discussed.

ACTIVITY   Issue copies of Figures 10.1 and 10.2 and ask the group, divided into smaller groups, to consider their usefulness as checklists, adding to, deleting or modifying items.

ACTIVITY   Consider the following situations and decide for each of them:

- What type of brief would you use?
- Would you use presentation aids?
- If so, what types of aids?
- Would you advise participants to take notes?
- Would you use handouts?
- If so, what type and extent of handout?
- What would be your *preferred* room and seating layout?
- How much time do you think would be the optimum? Minimum? Maximum?
- What would be your strategy for dealing with questions?

Assume that any equipment you require is available.

Situations

Report presentation on the progress of a project for which you are responsible to a meeting of senior managers. This presentation would take place during a half-day monthly meeting of the managers.

Pre-launch description of a new company product to 75 sales representatives and sales managers. This would be a specially arranged presentation.

Presentation of a new word-processing computer software program to a group of 15 of your own staff who are to start using it in a fortnight's time. You are responsible for the implementation and running of the program.

Presentation of the range of products produced by your company to an invited audience of past, present and potential customers. Sales have been falling in recent months.

As the machine-shop supervisor, you have to present to eight skilled machinists the new, very large, complex machines with multi-movement capabilities that are to be delivered the following week and which are revolutionary compared with existing machinery.

A presentation to the organization – 150 people – (excluding the senior managers) of the operational plan recently-produced by the senior manager group. This is in line with the requirements of Investors in People, an award which the organization is seeking.

11

Preparing Learner Presenters

This chapter:

- describes methods of giving presentation skill learners practice during a learning event
- outlines suggested presentation skill programmes.

PRESENTATION SKILLS PRACTICE

The comment has been made several times that effective presentation cannot be learned from a book which can only give information about the available and effective techniques and methods. This *must* be followed up by as much practice as possible before the first 'live' presentation is given, otherwise all the advice on controlling butterflies etc will disappear as soon as you step on to the stage.

The most effective way of getting this practice is attending a training course at which practice presentations are included with feedback following the performances. I feel that the minimum number of practice presentations is two or three: other opportunities can present themselves in addition to these more formal practices. The number of practices will obviously depend on the time available for the training and the format of the course, but the minimum of two or three should include an initial, diagnostic presentation, followed by a more substantial presentation following guidance on presentation techniques. A third might concentrate on presentations where two or more presenters are involved in the single presentation.

If the organization does not have the opportunity to provide a full training event, the absolute minimum should be the provision of time for practice presentations to be given, followed by expert feedback – a minimum of one presentation, but preferably two, the second giving the opportunity to take account of the feedback.

PRESENTATION PRACTICE APPROACHES

The first practice presentation should ideally be early in a training and development course. A short presentation – say ten minutes – could follow a summary description of some of the key factors for presentations. This presentation could be on any subject, the topic being left to the learner presenter. The participant should be advised prior to the event that they will be expected to give the presentation and it should be suggested that they do some initial preparation – research, visual aids, etc.

On the programme, time should be allocated for every participant to give their presentation in front of their fellow participants, either in front of the full group or in smaller groups if the main group is large. Following each presentation, feedback should be given by both the trainer or facilitator and the presenter's colleagues. A modified example of Figure 10.2 can be used, but the feedback should be 'soft', bearing in mind that this may be the first time that the person has spoken in front of a group. A video recording of the presentation can be helpful to the individual, who can either view it during the next presentation or at a later stage. But some direct feedback should be available, whether or not a video is used.

A second practice presentation should be planned for significantly later in the training, after all the advice and guidance sessions and activities have prepared the learner. Presenters can again be given the opportunity to choose their own subject, and the pre-event information should also give information about this second event and further suggestions offered on research and visual aids. Participants could collect specific objects – for example a bottle of whisky for a presentation on whisky distilling! They should, however, be advised not to produce a script or brief for the presentation, as time will be given during the event for this.

This second presentation could last 20 minutes, divided into sections by the presenter. If the programme can be arranged to allow it, the last afternoon (and evening) prior to the presentation should be made available for the participants to prepare their briefs and presentation aids. During this time, the trainer or facilitator should be available to give advice, guidance and help with the choice and production of aids.

Every participant should be given the opportunity to present, either to the full group or to smaller groups as necessary. Strict control should be kept over time, although not to the extent of green, yellow and red lights!

The competences questionnaire can (Figure 10.1) again be used for feedback, supplemented by video playback. The feedback at this stage, although critical in a positive manner, should pull few punches, particularly if this is the last practice session that will be available to the learner before a real event.

If any participant is to give a real presentation soon after the training event, the subject of this presentation can usefully be used for the practice session.

If there is time, there should be a third practice session. On this occasion the subject should be chosen for the presenter, and might be one in which the presenter is likely to be involved at work.

INFORMAL PRESENTATION PRACTICE

In addition to the formal presentation practice sessions, every opportunity should be given for more informal presentations, with the objective of giving participants every chance to increase their confidence in speaking before other people.

On a training course extending over several days, the use of a Learning Log is recommended.

A Learning Log is an instrument in which learners record, during a training event, and afterwards, their significant learning points in those events, for ease of recall. The Log consists of an introductory, explanatory page followed by a number of sheets in sets of three, one set for each day of the training event. It would normally be contained in a ring-binder.

Figures 11.1 to 11.4 suggest a suitable format for a Learning Logbook including an introduction.

A LEARNING LOG BOOK

KEEPING A LEARNING LOG

The objective of attending a learning event is to learn something you can use. A complex event can contain a number of ideas, activities etc that you might wish to implement at work. It can be difficult, particularly over an extended period, to remember all that you considered, perhaps even the important points.

A Learning Log:

- gives you a permanent document in which to record these ideas as they occur;
- helps you at a later stage to think about what you have experienced and learned, particularly the key ideas you want to retain;
- helps you consider at leisure which aspects you want to implement and how you are going to do this;
- is a reminder for you about your intentions when you get back to work;
- is a permanent record of your progress and development and of what you have learned.

If the other notes you may have taken and the handouts issued during the training programme are combined with this Log, you have a full record of your training to which you can refer at any time.

Your Learning Log should be completed frequently during the event – preferably during periods which may be allocated for this purpose – or during the evenings. Do not leave its completion any longer than this, otherwise there is the danger that some useful and/or important ideas or learning may be lost.

From your ongoing notes section, review these notes and select the ideas, techniques, suggestions and activities that you feel could be significant for you.

In the second section of the Log, describe these selections in as much detail as necessary so that you will be able to recall them later.

In the third section, preferably with a priority listing, describe, from your list in the second section, what you are going to implement or otherwise take action on.

- *What* are you going to do?
- *How* are you going to implement or action it?
- *When and/or by when* are you going to implement it?
- *What* resources will you need?
- *Who* can or needs to be involved?
- What implications are there for effects on others?

THE CONTINUED USE OF THE LEARNING LOG

On the training programme

At the start of the day following the one for which you have completed your Log you will, in a small group, be asked to describe the entries you have made. This presentation will:

(a) help you clarify your thoughts on the area presented;
(b) help you in the recall process;
(c) widen the views of the remainder of the group who may not have seen the implications of the areas you have highlighted;
(d) raise the opportunity for clarification.

As a continuous process

A Learning Log is not intended for use only on training programmes. We are learning all the time, in every type of situation, and a Log can help us capitalize on these opportunities. If you read a book and there are ideas that you want to remember and implement, enter these in your Log. If, in discussion with others, ideas come up that you feel may be of use to you, remember them and enter them in your Log at the first opportunity. Keep referring to your Log constantly to remind you of activities that you have not yet implemented.

Your line manager, in his or her process of your continuing assessment, will not only find your Log entries valuable in assessing your development, but could be impressed by your intent and persistence.

Remember that if eventually you decide to seek the award of the Training and Development National Vocational Qualification, this record can form a useful part of the portfolio you will need to produce.

Figure 11.1 *The introductory section of a Learning Log Book*

Set-sheet 1 can be used by the learner instead of or in addition to any notes that might be made during the training day of interesting, useful or significant learning points. See Figure 11.2.

DAY ONE

****

SET SHEET I

SECTION ONE

RUNNING RECORD OF ITEMS OF WHICH YOU WISH TO REMIND YOURSELF

xxxxxxxxxxxxxxxxxxxxxxxxxxxxxxxxxxxxxxxxxxxxxxxxxxxxxxxxxx

Figure 11.2 *Set-sheet 1 of a Learning Log Book*

Set-sheet 2 is used by learners to sort and summarize the points from sheet 1 that they particularly want to recall, perhaps adding references to handouts and other information. See Figure 11.3.

SET SHEET 2

SECTION TWO

DETAILED DESCRIPTIONS OF YOUR SELECTED ITEMS

xxxxxxxxxxxxxxxxxxxxxxxxxxxxxxxxxxxxxxxxxxxxxxxxxxxxxxxxxx

Figure 11.3 *Set-sheet 2 of a Learning Log Book*

Set-sheet 3 is a mini-action plan, detailing from sheet 2 entries that the learner particularly intends to implement and how, when etc this action will be taken. The various sheet 3s can be used in the formulation of the final action plan. See Figure 11.4.

```
┌─────────────────────────────────────────────────────────┐
│                                          SET SHEET 3      │
│                    SECTION THREE                          │
│                                                           │
│              IMPLEMENTATION DECISIONS                     │
│                                                           │
│  xxxxxxxxxxxxxxxxxxxxxxxxxxxxxxxxxxxxxxxxxxxxxxxxxxxxxxx   │
│                                                           │
└─────────────────────────────────────────────────────────┘
```

Figure 11.4 *Set-sheet 3 of a Learning Log Book*

The Log is issued at the start of the learning event and Set-sheets 2 and 3 are completed during the evenings, giving the learners an opportunity to reflect on the events of the day and their significance.

The next morning, ideally in groups of six, each member presents to the rest of the group and a facilitator what they have entered in their Log, why they have made these entries and what they intend to do about them. Use can also be made of activities or buzz groups, from which a report is made to the full learning group. Although these are not specifically designed for presentation skills practice, a few minutes can usefully be spent in seeking the views of the individual (and others) on how they felt they had presented their reports.

CO-PRESENTING PRACTICE

On occasions it is necessary for a presentation to be made by more than one person, for example using various experts, or perhaps it is useful for a team to make a presentation about something that has involved the whole team.

A multi-presenter event requires even more planning and practise than an individual presentation. Planning the material for the complete presentation should present little difficulty, but the division of roles can be complicated. Any 'expert' member will act as presenter for these items, with one person (perhaps the team leader) acting as the linker and introducer of each person and section. If there are no 'experts' part of the planning will be deciding who does what, but it is always useful to have one member as the linker, introducer and time controller.

Extreme care has to be taken to ensure that multi-presentations run smoothly, but they can be very successful, particularly as the change of presenter introduces variety and extends the normally limited attention span.

PRESENTATION SKILLS TRAINING PROGRAMMES

This book is intended to provide much of the material necessary to produce presentation skills training and development programmes, probably more than can be included in the time available. However, it is for the provider of the training to select the most suitable material that can be covered in the available time, bearing in mind that the most important aspect is the presentation practice and feedback. The time factor is critical, and programme planners must argue strongly for the maximum amount of time. Obviously, if the people concerned are fairly experienced presenters who only require a refresher, the time can be minimal, most of it being taken up with a discussion of problems encountered and suggestions to counter these, plus practice present-ations with critical feedback. A complete beginner in presentations will obviously require softer and more extensive treatment, and will need the time to learn most of the material in this book.

When time for inexperienced presenters is limited, valuable use of pre-event tasks and reading can be made, so that on the event itself much of the input material will be in the form of confirming of understanding of the techniques and practices, with skills practice again being the principal activity.

There is little justification for running a one-day training course in presentation skills for large numbers of people which excludes practical work. These usually consist of a series of input sessions by facile presenters and little real learning takes place.

SUGGESTED TRAINING PROGRAMMES

1. Refresher programme for experienced or semi-experienced presenters

Duration

One-day workshop

Membership

Six participants per one trainer or facilitator – more than this number will require too many presentations within the same group, which will become boring and ineffective. If the number must be more than six, two trainers should be available, each taking charge of a small group.

Pre-course tasks

All participants should read a publication on presentation skills (for example, this book, concentrating particularly on the boxed summaries and detail of techniques of which they are not aware or are not sure about).

Advise participants that they will be required to conduct a 20-minute presentation on a subject of their own choice, for which they should prepare a brief and any aids required.

Programme

Introduction of the workshop and self-introductions of the participants – these can be assessed as mini-presentations.
Review of the key presentation techniques or those identified by the participants as being required.
Time for participants to finalize their presentations.
(If the workshop commences at 9 am, with one hour for lunch and two 15-minute refreshment breaks, this first section of the programme should be completed before 11 am, ready for the presentation practices to commence).
Presentation practice for each participant. The timing will be approximately:

    5 minutes between each presentation for setting-up the next one;
    20 minutes maximum presentation time;
    20 minutes feedback, including completion of feedback questionnaires (self and audience). Most of the feedback should be given by the presenters themselves and the audience with the facilitator only adding any important aspect omitted.

Total presentation time, say 6 x 45 minutes =
4 hours 30 minutes plus some slippage time.
Final review.

Although I have described this as a one-day workshop, even if six members per trainer are involved, it will be obvious that one day is tight for an effective workshop, a more realistic timing being one and a half days.

2. Programme for inexperienced learners or presenters with limited experience

Duration

Two-day workshop

Membership

Six participants per one trainer or facilitator – more than this number will require too many presentations within the same group; this will become boring and ineffective. If the numbers are greater than six, two trainers should be available, each taking charge of a small group.

Pre-course tasks

All participants should read a publication on presentation skills (for example, this book, concentrating particularly on the boxed summaries and detail of techniques of which they are not aware or are not sure about).

Advise participants that they will be required to conduct a 10-minute and a 20-minute presentation on subjects of their own choice, for which they should prepare a brief (outline only for the 20-minute presentation) and any aids required.

Programme

Day one

Introduction of the workshop and self-introductions of the participants – these can be assessed as mini-presentations.   30 min
Review of the key preparation techniques or those identified by the participants; practice activity.   60 min
Presentation practice for the 10-minute presentations for each participant.
The timing will be approximately:
   5 minutes between each presentation for setting-up the next one;
   10 minutes maximum presentation time;
   15 minutes feedback, including completion of feedback questionnaires (self and audience). Most of the feedback should be given by the presenters themselves and the audience with the facilitator only adding any important aspect omitted.
   Total presentation time, say 6 x 30 minutes =
   3 hours plus some slippage time.   3 hours 15 min

Review of the key presentation techniques selected (from this book), with practice activities, and guided by the mini-presentations' achievements.   60 min

Review of the key techniques for constructing and using the most common visual aids   30 min

Time for participants to finalize their 20-minute presentations – final preparation of brief and construction of visual aids. Full resources should be made available and on a residential event the trainer or facilitator should be available if the participants want to continue their preparation during the evening.

Participants should also be asked to complete during the evening a Learning Log, issued and described at the start of the workshop.

Day two

Log Book: Each member should make a brief presentation on their Log entries and why these were made.   45 min

Review (brief) of key presentation skills not covered on the previous day or any identified from Log presentations.   30 min

Preparation: Final preparation time for presentations.   30 min

20-minute presentation practice for each participant. The timing will be approximately:

   5 minutes between each presentation for setting-up the next one;

   20 minutes maximum presentation time;

   20 minutes feedback, including completion of feedback questionnaires (self and audience). Most of the feedback should be given by the presenters themselves and the audience with the facilitator only adding any important aspect omitted.

   Total presentation time, say 6 x 45 minutes =

   4 hours 30 minutes plus some slippage time.   4 hours 45 min

Final review of lessons learned, end-of-event evaluation and action planning in conjunction with final Learning Log completion.   45 min

3. Programme for inexperienced or presenters with limited experience

Duration

Three-day workshop

Membership

Six per one trainer or facilitator – more than this number will require too many presentations within the same group; this will become boring and ineffective. If the numbers are greater than six, two trainers should be available, each taking charge of a small group.

Pre-course tasks

All participants should read a publication on presentation skills (for example, this book, concentrating particularly on the boxed summaries and detail of techniques of which they are not aware or are not sure about).

Advise participants that they will be required to conduct a 10-minute and a 20-minute presentation on subjects of their own choice for which they should prepare a brief (outline only for the 20-minute presentation) and any aids required.

Programme

Day one
Introduction of the workshop and self-introductions of the participants – these can be assessed as mini-presentations. Other forms of introduction activities can be used.   30 min
Review of the key aspects of communication, using the material in this book and others that concentrate on general communication barriers, models and techniques. Use appropriate activities.   1 hour 15 min
Review of communication barriers, models and techniques, both verbal and non-verbal. Activities related to these topics.   2 hours
Presentation practice for the 10-minute presentations for each participant. The timing will be approximately:
  5 minutes between each presentation for setting-up the next one;
  10 minutes maximum presentation time;

15 minutes feedback, including completion of feedback questionnaires (self and audience). Most of the feedback should be given by the presenters themselves and the audience with the facilitator only adding any important aspect omitted.

Total presentation time, say 6 x 30 minutes =
3 hours plus some slippage time.   3 hours 15 min

Evening task: Participants should be asked to complete the first stage of their Learning Log during the evening.

Day two

Log Book: Each member should make a brief presentation on their Log entries and why these were made.   45 min

Review of the key brief preparation techniques with practice in two methods – eg horizontal and patterned note.   1 hour 30 min

Review of the key presentation techniques selected (from this book), with practice activities, and guided by the mini-presentations' achievements.   60 min

Review of the key techniques for constructing and using the visual aids that are available to presenters. Practice in constructing different forms of visual or audio aid and presenting these to the group.   2 hours

Time for participants to finalize their 20-minute presentations – final preparation of brief and construction of visual aids. Full resources should be made available and on a residential event the trainer or facilitator should be available if the participants want to continue their preparation during the evening.

Evening task: Participants should be asked to complete the second section of their Learning Log during the evening.

Day three

Log Book: Each member should make brief presentation on their Log entries and why these were made.   45 min

Review (brief) of key presentation skills not covered on the previous day or any identified from Log presentations.   30 min

Preparation: Final preparation time for presentations   30 min

20-minute presentation practice for each participant. The timing will be approximately:

  5 minutes between each presentation set for setting-up the
  next one;

20 minutes maximum presentation time;
20 minutes feedback, including completion of feedback
questionnaires (self and audience). Most of the feedback
should be given by the presenters themselves and the
audience with the facilitator only adding any important
aspect omitted.
Total presentation time, say 6 x 45 minutes =
4 hours 30 minutes plus some slippage time.   4 hours 45 min
Final review of lessons learned, end-of-event
evaluation and action planning in conjunction with
final Learning Log completion.   45 min

Obviously there are many other variations. Workshops can include
more or less on communication, learning and listening; spend more or
less time on reviews of the various techniques or on using activities
(but only less as a last resort, as more is learned from relevant activities
than from any other method). More practice can be given in co- or
multi-presenting, again including time for discussion of the techniques
used and the presenters' preparation.

The variations will depend on the time available, the existing
knowledge or skills level of the presenters and the extent and depth of
the material you need to include. Include as much practice as possible
and, as suggested earlier, include an appropriate number of practical
activities.

THE FINAL REHEARSAL

You are now approaching your first real presentation: having learned
as much as you can about presentations from the literature and a
training workshop, you have analysed the audience and all the
environmental factors; and you have planned and prepared your
presentation material, your aids and brief. Even armed with all this
knowledge you would be wise to take one further step before the fateful
day – rehearse. Four main approaches are possible for rehearsing (not
rehearsal, as you may require more than one).

1. in front of a full length mirror;
2. using a cassette audio recorder;
3. using a video camcorder;
4. gathering a group of colleagues to act as your audience.

Whichever of these approaches you use, your objectives are to:

- practise your presentation skills;
- validate your material content;
- confirm the timing of your presentation;
- in the fourth approach, practise handling questions.

The fourth approach will be the most effective as far as receiving independent feedback is concerned, although gathering such a group is not always possible. Use a feedback questionnaire such as the one shown in Figure 10.1 and seek the most searching criticism you can. Kindness may not be the most effective feedback, particularly if you repeat an ineffective approach with your next, real audience.

Using a mirror is probably the least effective, feedback being only temporary and very subjective – you may even spend too much time admiring yourself! But it has its uses if no other means are available.

Audio recording and playback are very useful for your oral techniques feedback, although remember that, unless you are recording with professional material in a properly constructed studio, your recorded voice pitch, tone and volume are at the mercy of the quality of the microphone and recorder. It is a very useful method, however, for highlighting your verbal mannerisms.

A video recording with a home camcorder is simply arranged and has the added advantage that your non-verbal signals as well as your verbal ones can be identified and assessed, and you can assess your use of your training aids. Although it will be a subjective self-assessment, you will find the Figure 10.1 questionnaire a useful aid while you are watching the video. It will concentrate your mind on what you are doing, rather than leaving you free to be mesmerized by your image.

A useful tip is to try to replicate as closely as possible the real life situation. Don't be tempted to sit or stand too near the microphone(s) as would probably happen if you follow the recording equipment technical advice. Stand away from the mike so that you have to project your voice as you would in the presentation room.

Now go ahead and present – good luck and enjoy your presentations! Don't forget to review your performance when it is all over.

Appendix:
The Presentation Development Process

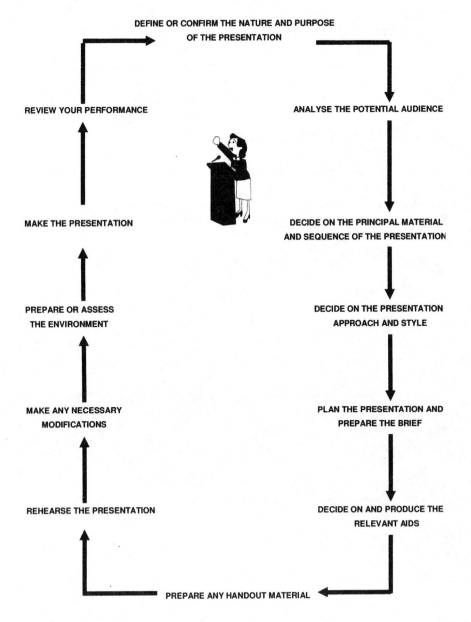

DEFINE OR CONFIRM THE NATURE AND PURPOSE
OF THE PRESENTATION

REVIEW YOUR PERFORMANCE

ANALYSE THE POTENTIAL AUDIENCE

MAKE THE PRESENTATION

DECIDE ON THE PRINCIPAL MATERIAL
AND SEQUENCE OF THE PRESENTATION

PREPARE OR ASSESS
THE ENVIRONMENT

DECIDE ON THE PRESENTATION
APPROACH AND STYLE

MAKE ANY NECESSARY
MODIFICATIONS

PLAN THE PRESENTATION AND
PREPARE THE BRIEF

REHEARSE THE PRESENTATION

DECIDE ON AND PRODUCE THE
RELEVANT AIDS

PREPARE ANY HANDOUT MATERIAL

Recommended Reading

Bradbury, Andrew (1995) *Successful Presentation Skills*, Kogan Page.

Buzan, Tony (1988) *Use Your Head (rev edn)*, Ariel Books, BBC Books.

Cotton, Julie (1995) *The Theory of Learning*, Kogan Page.

Denham, Wendy and Naylor, Elizabeth (1995) *30 Training Sessions (Activities) for Effective Presentations*, Gower.

Fenwick, Mike (1994) *Presentation Skills: 20 Tried and Tested Training Activities for Making Effective Presentations*, Fenman.

Flegg, David and McHale, Josephine (1991) *Selecting and Using Training Aids*, Kogan Page.

Forsyth, Patrick (1992) *Running an Effective Training Session*, Gower.

Gilgrist, David with Davies, Rex (1996) *Winning Presentations*, Gower.

Hamlin, Sonya (1989) *How to Talk So People Listen*, Thorsons.

Honey, Peter and Mumford, Alan (1992) *A Manual of Learning (3rd edn)*, Peter Honey Publications.

James, Judi (1995) *Body Talk: The Skills of Positive Image*, The Industrial Society.

James, Roger (1995) *The Techniques of Instruction*, Gower.

Rae, Leslie (1994) *The Trainer Development Programme, Volumes 1 and 2*, Kogan Page.

Rae, Leslie (1995) *Techniques of Training (3rd edn)*, Gower.

Rae, Leslie (1996) *Using Activities in Training and Development*, Kogan Page.

Rae, Leslie (1997) *Training Aids: A Complete Resource Kit for Training and Development*, Kogan Page.

Sampson, Eleri (1994) *The Image Factor*, Kogan Page.

Sampson, Eleri (1996) *101 Ways to Make a Professional Impact*, Kogan Page.

Thorne, Kaye and Mackey, David (1996) *Everything You Ever Needed to Know about Training*, Kogan Page.

Townsend, John (1997) *The Business Presenter's Pocketbook (6th edn)*, Management Pocketbooks.

Audio and Video Resources

Townsend, John *Tips for Presenters*, audio cassette, Management
Pocketbooks, 1992.
Townsend, John *Memories are Made of This*, video, Melrose, 1994
(problems of memory and recall with suggested solutions).
Townsend, John *Ten Training Tips*, video, Melrose, 1994.
Pease, Allan *Body Language*, video, Gower, 1987.
Pease, Allan *Silent Signals*, video, Gower, 1989.
The Floor is Yours, Now, video, Connaught Training (Gower), 1987
(planning, preparing and delivering a presentation).
The Audience is Yours, Now, video, Connaught Training (Gower), 1992
(handling audiences).

The videos listed above not only describe the relevant subject areas
but also demonstrate three different presenter styles that can be used
for discussion during a programme.

Index